The Wakes Resorts

RON AND MARLENE FREETHY

Foreword

Ron and Marlene Freethy have written one of the most interesting and compelling books about The Wakes holiday towns that I have ever had the pleasure of reading. Although I have, earlier in my life, visited each of the towns featured, after reading the book I now have a great urge to return to each place and wander about . . . with an opened copy of their work ready for me to refer to.

Who ever thought that New Brighton, with its "Ham and Eggs Terrace", was the favourite resort of Liverpool and Lancashire trippers and roughs? The writings of Sulley in 1889 suggests that! I've learned that, on the Sunday following St. Cuthbert's Eve in August 1219, "folks travelled some distance to tear off their clothes and frolic in the sea" at Southport.

Lovely Lytham, Super St. Annes, Boisterous Blackpool, Thornton, Cleveleys, Fleetwood, Morecambe and Heysham — they write about them all. They tell us in detail the history of our Lancashire seaside resorts, those magic places of entertainment that have contributed to the prosperity of Britain and the enjoyment of the holidaymakers.

Their magic pen has vividly drawn a most interesting Lancashire coastline that will give knowledge and pleasure to all who read this fascinating and historical work.

DAME THORA HIRD, OBE

Introduction

For more than thirty years we have been presenting programmes for television and radio about the coastline of north-western England. In the early period it was hard to be optimistic, but by the mid 1980s some improvements were being attempted. However, there were far too many thorns among the fragrant roses.

Some ten years ago we produced a small book about the resorts and Dame Thora Hird was kind enough to write a foreword. This lady has been a great ambassador for the area, and she must be delighted to see the progress being made.

During 1995 and 1996, whilst working for BBC local radio stations, we set out to discover more and more of the exciting developments which are taking place throughout the region. We are grateful to our BBC colleagues, especially Evelyn Draper of Merseyside and John Clayton of Lancashire.

We are also grateful for the help and encouragement given by the editors of the Evening Gazette at Blackpool, the Bolton Evening News and especially to Peter Butterfield, Alan Simpson and Lynn Ashwell of the Lancashire Evening Telegraph.

Thanks are also due to the very many listeners and readers who contributed their memories to the history of the various resorts.

The relationship between the politicians and tourism officers and the media has also improved and we are grateful to Jim Trotman of Morecambe, Mike Chadwick of Blackpool,

Mrs. V. Wood of Lytham St. Annes and to Philip King of Southport. Michael Brown, the Chief Executive of the Wyre Borough Council, was generous with his time as was the staff of the Fleetwood Museum, with Simon Heyhoe an ever-ready source of information.

Our thanks are due to John Clayton of BBC Radio Lancashire who gave great assistance during the production of a series of six one-hour documentaries on the Wakes Resorts.

The best way by far to see the region as a whole is to look down upon it from the air, so Robert Jones of Lytham took us up in his balloon and on landing entertained us with a glass of champagne.

Our thanks are also due to the many friends who were both generous with their time and the provision of archive photographs.

RON & MARLENE FREETHY

CHAPTER ONE:

Wakes Towns

A 'wake' originally meant a funeral, and as this was often an excuse for a party not everyone was sad. In the days when travel was not easy, a death was often the only reason for a family get-together. When rich men died their passing was often used as an excuse for their work people to be given a day off or even two. Some historians suggest that a Wake referred to a rush-bearing, when vegetation was strewn on the floors of churches before they were paved with stone. All the people got to work cutting, carrying and laying the rushes and when the job was finished a holiday was celebrated.

When the textile workers were first given holidays it was initially a few days, which only later became a wakes week. When the mills were working full blast the holiday period provided a chance to clean boilers and sweep and repair chimneys, which were at this time called "smoke pokes", seemingly an ideal name. Industrialists realised that to have every mill in the region idle at the same time made no economic sense. The idea of staggered holidays for each town was thus born and the Bolton week would be followed by Burnley and then by Blackburn. The skilled cleaners and repairers could thus move from town to town and the seaside resorts could also cope with the gradual and continual stream of eager visitors, rather than having them all descend upon them at once.

This system worked very smoothly until two weeks paid holiday became the rule and a degree of overlapping had to take place. We have both spent our lives living and working in the Wakes towns and regularly went to the coast to relax. For a period, we lived in Burnley and worked in Bolton and our holidays, therefore, became somewhat confused. We lived on a hill outside Burnley and watched the Wakes Seaside Specials steaming out of the station. We then watched spellbound as the smoke cleared from the hundred or more mill chimneys and we realised just why the Victorians called them smoke pokes. We did our washing and hung it up on the line, relaxing in the knowledge that because there was no soot in the air we would have the cleanest laundry of the year.

Our fathers were 'twisters', skilled twisters of cotton yarn who spent their working lives in the mills. Once their Christmas dinner had been digested they set about planning "Burnley Fair" and calculated how much of their weekly holiday fund would have accumulated by the time they arrived to board the train or the coach. When they could afford a car the family still planned the holiday savings by having weekly collections docked from their pay by the office of each mill.

Each of the textile towns had its own character and each had a preference for one of the seaside resorts, although Blackpool was always the most popular. Before considering the six resorts of New Brighton (as we had Liverpool connections), Southport and Lytham St. Annes (if we felt posh), Blackpool (when we felt like letting our hair down) and Fleetwood and Morecambe, we need to take a brief look at the Wakes towns themselves which ensured that Cotton was crowned the undisputed King of Industry.

Accrington

Accrington was once famous for its fine linen and for the production of Ewbank carpet cleaners, which were first produced by Richard Kenyon in the 1860s. It also had a couple of interesting American connections in that Butch Cassidy, who became famous along with the Sundance Kid, was born in Burnley but went to school in Accrington before emigrating to the States. Another important American export was baseball bats which were once produced in the busy little town.

The name Accrington meant, the settlement among the oak trees, as *Ac* also derives from the fruit of the tree which is, of course, the acorn. Another settlement derived from the same root was Acton, now in London but once an independent and very rural village.

The area around Accrington belonged from Norman times until the Dissolution of the Monasteries in 1538 to Kirkstall Abbey near Leeds. The town later earned its living from coal, cotton, glass, snooker tables and bricks. Many of the young men of the area were killed during the World War I when their regiment, which was known as the Accrington Pals, was slaughtered on the Somme in 1916. This meant that after the war there was a shortage of weavers which was

Accrington in 1899 — the tram lines can be seen. We often wonder where the people seen in this photograph spent their Wakes Week.

traditionally a man's job, so women had to take their place. During World War II the town also played a vital role, with the Ewbank factory being adapted to produce parts for aeroplanes and gliders, many of which flew to Arnhem and to the battle areas of Normandy. Around 1940 a huge barrage balloon was tethered over the strategically important railway bridge, which has since been renovated.

We have always enjoyed our visits to Accrington market which has retained all its Victorian elegance and has changed little in character since 1899.

Bacup

We have happy memories of Bacup as we have often given lectures to the 'Bacup Nats' and produced radio programmes with the world famous coconut dancers. One of our uncles was a brass band player of some renown and he told us that the Irwell Springs

Band at Bacup won the Brass Band Championship of Great Britain three times at the prestigious venue of London's Crystal Palace.

The river Irwell rises from Thieveley Park between Bacup and Burnley and it is this river which gives the town its character. The Pike is 1,474 feet (449 metres) high and at 1,250 feet (381 metres) Sharneyford Mill was the highest mill in the country. Even the town centre, which actually seems to be in a dip, is more than 800 feet (244 metres) above sea level.

Bacup fared particularly badly during the decline of the cotton industry, but the brave town has never lost its sense of humour or its pride.

The 'Nats' or 'Naturalists' are notoriously friendly leg-pullers and their museum, which previously served as a pub and a doss house, on Yorkshire Street is now crammed with the town's history. There are hundreds of photographs all filed lovingly away, and there are cases and drawers full of natural history specimens and artefacts collected since the Society was founded in the 1870s. There is even a working loom, and outside in the small garden area street signs have been collected and thus preserved for posterity. Many of the 'Nats' have made detailed studies of the hillside coal mines and cotton mills in the valley bottoms, and also, the local churches and chapels. It is fitting that the hymn tune 'Bacup' should be composed by the Reverend Roscoe, the vicar of Christ Church.

The Nutters dance is in complete contrast, and may be pagan in origin but perhaps dating back to the crusades. The 'Nutters' are an all-male Morris dancing troup but many historians think that Moorish Dancers would be a more accurate description, especially as the troup black their faces.

Blackburn

In contrast to Bacup, which developed slowly into a busy small town, Blackburn developed quickly from a textile based village to a massive town and one of the dominant princes in the realm of King Cotton. Those who work hard also learned to play hard during their limited leisure period, so Blackburn Wakes Week was eagerly awaited by the north-western seaside resorts who anticipated the workers' excursion trains carrying those only too eager to have a "reet good time," and willing to part with hard earned brass. A friend's father always put a red ten-shilling note in a tobacco tin and buried it in "t' coil oil". The heap of coal concealed the following week's rent and food money because he knew he would be skint when he got home.

Blackburn has done more than its share to write the history of Lancashire's cotton industry, with James Hargreaves of nearby Oswaldtwistle playing a major role. Whilst living at Rose Cottage, which is now the sub-post office at Stanhill, James began to wonder if it was possible to make a mass produced spinning machine, and in 1764 he succeeded. It has been known ever since as the 'Spinning Jenny' with the usual explanation being that Hargreaves' daughter, or perhaps his wife, called Jenny accidentally upended her

July, 1945: Blackburn folk queue for the Blackpool train — their first 'wakes' holiday since the war. Note the election posters with Barbara Castle on course to represent the town.

spinning wheel. James then realised that in that position several wheels could be turned by a single operator. A more scientific explanation suggests that, in the Lankie twang of the time, any strange machine was actually known as a 'jinny' and was said to be inspired and operated by a local boggart named Jinny Greenteeth.

This little area of Lancashire seemed to breed innovators, as one of Hargreaves' co-workers — perhaps apprentice scientists would have been a better term for them — was the grandfather of Robert Peel, and who was also called Robert but affectionately known as "Owld Parsley Peel". He got his name because he traced parsley leaves onto cloth to create a pattern. His little cottage at Peel Fold close to Stanhill was a hive of industry as he experimented with calico printing which eventually made the family fortune. This later proved to be useful to Robert Peel whose affluence enabled him to become Prime Minister and he was later knighted. This was, however, long after the family had 'flit' to Bury but he never forgot his roots.

We have had many long conversations with Maggie Simms, the curator of Blackburn museum, and she has helped us to trace the history of Blackburn, which once stood on the banks of the pure Blakewater which is a tributary of the river Darwen. Was the river named because the burn was indeed black and peat-stained, or was the name a corruption of bleach-water because the flax which preceded cotton was actually bleached? This was processed around the stream as long ago as Anglo-Saxon times. We shall probably never know the certain answer, but what is very easily traced is the phenomenal growth in cotton which took place in the town, and which resulted in the rivers being culverted to allow more houses and mills to be built. The Blakewater now passes unseen beneath Blackburn's new shopping centre.

Progress may have been quick but it was far from smooth, and James Hargreaves was not a popular chap, as his Jenny was soon shown to do the work of six! He had to flee to Nottingham to carry, on his work and later on, in 1826, and despite the presence of soldiers, a mob of 10,000 took sledgehammers and battered the improved looms into splinters. Plaques placed on modern buildings have been erected to mark the sites of these sad, yet historic, events.

As the population increased to beyond 100,000 and factories sprouted like mushrooms, smoke and chemical pollution reached epidemic proportions. The Fielden family actually deserted their one-time idyllic Pleasington Hall by the banks of the Darwen because of pollution and went to live in Scarborough. The cotton operatives, however, had to stay where they were, and even used Pleasington Hall as a "pleasure garden". During one blessed period of the year the Wakes Week meant freedom from muck, and happiness at the seaside could be guaranteed until brass and time ran out!

Darwen

This splendid little town lies under the shadow of Blackburn, but it has a distinguished history of its own. It even had a football league team which briefly was able to beat the Rovers of Blackburn. The town still has some wonderful old textile buildings especially India Mill, with the whole settlement being set in a valley dominated by Darwen Tower which was built in 1897 to commemorate the Diamond Jubilee of Queen Victoria's coronation.

India Mill has something of an Italian feel to it but its name shows that for many years Darwen's textiles were exported to India. In the 1930s Ghandi undertook a fact finding tour as the guest of Percy Davies a local mill owner. When independence came in 1947 it was obvious that India would start to produce its own cotton cloth and cut out the middle-man. This was one of the major reasons for the eventual decline in the Lancashire cotton industry but although the 'boom' has, so to speak, gone 'bang' there are many "Darreners" who still have fond memories of the cotton workers' wakes and of the bellman who called the time of the trains to ensure nobody was late.

Thomas Greenwood, photographed in the 1890s, was Darwen's last bellman.

Bolton

Children of the forties and fifties, like us, had a much easier life than did our parents. The Education Act of 1944 made good parents realise that "them wee brains could mek good". We depended upon our parents to make sacrifices and off we went to be 'edicated' and teach school. We never, however, forgot the sounds, sights and smells of the mills and when we started teaching in Bolton we knew about the life of working families and their ambitions for their children. We knew also that Bolton had a long and distinguished history and that it greeted its wakes holiday as a ray of bright warm sunshine. These traditions thankfully remain, and nobody here will ever accept that Bolton-le-Moors, as it was once called, is in Greater Manchester. Greater nothing — Bolton is Bolton, it is great on its own and it is in Lancashire!

The village of Bolton was indeed set on the moors and it was engaged in the textile trade, which was then based upon wool and linen, from 1337 and probably for a long time prior to this. The first written record was because of the exodus of Flemish weavers, some of whom settled in Bolton. Some 'amateur' historians have suggested that the 'Sabot' footwear they brought with them was the origin of the Lancashire clog, but many of the 'experts' in this field point out that wooden footwear was in use from Saxon times. Who cares, but many Bolton lads and lasses can still remember the clatter of clogs on the cobbled streets as folk made the then short journey between home and mill. They each made a modest contribution towards the wages of the 'knocker-up' who had a list of clients and the shift they operated.

In recent years we have contributed articles to the Bolton Evening News whose offices are overlooked by the splendid parish church of St. Peters, which had to be rebuilt around 1860, but the architect sensibly copied his design to comply with the fourteenth-century blueprint. The church has played its part in the events of history and Bolton lads gathered there before setting off to join Sir Edward Stanley's forces at Flodden. In 1513 these rawboned troops routed the Scots.

A later Stanley painted a much darker side to Bolton's history and he was executed in the market square as the townsfolk took their revenge upon him. In 1644 during the height of the Civil War, Bolton stood firm for Parliament but the Earl of Derby, who was a Stanley, was a King's man. On 28th May a Royalist army led by Prince Rupert and Stanley, at the head of a much superior force, attacked Bolton and gave no quarter to anyone as hundreds of people, many of them being non-combatants, were slaughtered. When Cromwell eventually overthrew King Charles I, Stanley fled to the Isle of Man. In 1651 the Earl returned with Charles II and attempted to restore the monarchy, but the Battle of Worcester was lost. Stanley was captured, brought to Bolton and after a night spent at the 'Old Man and the Scythe' he was executed at the town cross. A memorial to these bloody events has since been erected. This also celebrates other events in the busy industrial life of Bolton.

A chapter of the history of cotton can also be written here, as opposite the cross was once the barber's shop of Richard Arkwright, whilst Samuel Crompton also made his textile machinery innovations when living in the town.

Richard Arkwright (1732–92) had humble origins but during his busy life he earned his knighthood by hard work and a high degree of 'business acumen'. Unlike most inventors who forged the Industrial Age, Richard was not naive and was quite prepared to steal ideas from other people, having his eye firmly on making his fortune. Born in 1732, the thirteenth child of a Preston tailor, young Richard went to Bolton where he was apprenticed to a barber but soon became an expert wig-maker using "natural" hair and was much in demand throughout Lancashire.

It was, however, as an innovator of textile machinery that he achieved lasting fame and he set up a workshop in a house near Preston's Parish church of St. Peter's. In 1769, he built his now famous Water Frame but the local artisans made life so uncomfortable for the man whose machine could do the work of eight without getting tired, that like Hargreaves he moved to Nottingham. There Richard Arkwright achieved fame and made his fortune. His talents should be celebrated by the setting up of a museum in Preston and Arkwright's House would be ideal. It still stands but looks rather run-down. It is, however, being restored as a conference centre but would be ideal as a museum and we would be the first to celebrate with a glass of the bubbly if this came to pass.

Crompton is much more of a Bolton lad and his birthplace at Fir Fold still stands, whilst on the opposite side of what is now a modern and busy road called Crompton Way stands Hall i' th' Wood, which in Samuel's day was just that!

Samuel was born in 1753 and although a genius of invention he was no businessman. In 1779, he invented the spinning mule whilst living at Hall i' th' Wood, which is a half timbered manor house. This address was not so prestigious as it sounds because it was then divided into a number of tenements rented by poor folk. By 1899 the hall was derelict but it was bought and renovated as a museum by Lord Leverhulme who was born in Bolton under the name of William Hesketh Lever. Much of his fortune, made from the manufacture of soap, was used to benefit his home town, while at nearby Rivington he laid out his personal estate. He did, however, allow access to the workers thus providing them with a breath of fresh air over the weekend, but was no substitute for a week away at the seaside!

Burnley, Nelson, Colne

Home for us has almost always been in and around the valley of the Lancashire Calder and its tributaries. We have seen King Cotton being forced to abdicate during the period when the Wakes holiday became concentrated upon the Spanish Costas. Only recently has there been any revival of interest in the history of the cotton industry and the Wakes Seaside Resorts which provided the mill folk with their well earned rest.

Burnley's textile history is well told in the Towneley Hall museum, the Weavers Triangle Visitors Centre and at Queen Street Mill which, although partly a museum, still sells its traditionally woven garments using the power of steam.

Burnley has not forgotten its traditions when it really was the cotton weaving centre of the world and its specialism was in the printing of calico. In 1913 more than 100,000 looms were operating, in 1914 Burnley beat Liverpool 1-0 in the Cup Final and soon after went to war. One of our grandfathers went to the trenches of France and did not come back, the other slaved away producing the essential textiles and later became a respected mill manager. Jimmy Jaques may well have had ancestors who came from

Huguenot stock who escaped persecution in France by flitting to Burnley and thus added essential skills and influenced local traditions. Jimmy would certainly have recognised Queen Street Mill still driven by steam and the only one left operating in England.

During a recording of a Radio Lancashire programme on the Leeds to Liverpool Canal we talked to Mr Brian Hall, who has had much to do with the setting up of the Weavers Triangle Visitors' Centre. This was once the canal toll house set among a network of old mills which from 1996 onwards are being restored and will become restaurants and shops, which is a far better way of celebrating history than allowing them to fall down. Brian Hall told us why Burnley's wakes holiday became known as Burnley Fair. Not everybody could afford to go away and during the break from work a fun fair was held; the Visitors' Centre has a working model of a typical scene. The fair still comes to town and so does the 'Pot Fair' where many a bargain can be had from the swift talking stall holders who are a subtle combination of vendors of pottery and skilled jugglers.

Most folk in the town, however, preferred to juggle their brass in one of the wakes resorts. We vividly remember our parents' reactions to a two week holiday. One week might be spent in Devon, Cornwall or perhaps Scotland whilst the second week would be spent in Blackpool or perhaps on a series of day trips to take in most of the

The knocker-upper — a familiar sight in the Lancashire Wakes Towns. This is a picture taken in Burnley during the 1880s.

wakes resorts. This could be done either by taking the car or by giving the old banger a rest from the long holiday and purchasing a "run about" rail ticket, which allowed unlimited travel for five, six or even seven days.

Nelson and Colne are usually regarded these days as mere satellites to Burnley but this is quite unfair as both have an important history of their own.

The word Nelson did not exist until after a railway halt was constructed close to the Lord Nelson pub, and the town later took on the name of the station. Prior to this there were two small villages called Great and Little Marsden, which both earned their living from textiles from at least the fifteenth century. Later, Edge End and Lomeshaye (pronounced Lomishaw) Mills played their part in the Industrial Revolution, first being powered by water and then by steam. A well designed park set around Marsden Hall became something of a 'lung' for the cotton operatives, and for those who could not afford to go away for the wakes the open air swimming pool made many forget their lack of liquid assets, especially during a heat wave.

"Bonny Colne upon the hill" earns both descriptions — it has a bonny history and its lovely old parish church is set high on a hill.

Colne had a market charter as early as 1296, but there is evidence of a Roman fort at Castercliffe on a hill above the town. Most historians feel that the history of the fort is even earlier, and Iron Age fortifications can still be seen. St. Bartholomew's church is Norman. In the grounds of the former library, which is now a chapel, the datestone of the Piece Hall can still be found and nearby is a memorial to Wallace Hartley the bandmaster of the ill-fated Titanic who bravely conducted his orchestra as the liner sank. Wallace was born in the town. We once spoke to David Kerr who was an apprentice blacksmith in 1912 and who remembered the news of the disaster reaching the mill town. The shock caused him to slip and cut his arm. He bore the scar to his dying day.

Bury

This now busy town, set on the banks of the much-maligned Irwell, once had a castle overlooking the river bank and the unpolluted water was full of salmon and trout. Although it was a cruel sport, the stretch of the river Irwell hereabouts was said to be the best otter hunting country in England.

What happened to the town and the river? The answer is in one word — industry. The Irwell became so polluted that few dare go near it and the industry which caused it spread so quickly that Bury and the then quite separate village of Manchester merged into one continuous urban sprawl. What remained intact was the character of the people, whose ancestors were hand loom weavers who had come down from their cottages on the hills to create the wealth of England and to help crown King Cotton. Their wakes holiday was part of their inheritance because their ancestors had been well used to lungs full of fresh air as they laboured high up in the hills of the Irwell Valley.

It was a Bury lad by the name of John Kay who made a giant step in the technology of textiles by inventing the flying shuttle. This invention has been reliably dated to 1733 and it speeded up weaving to such a degree that England dominated the textile industry of the world for around 200 years. He well deserves his memorial in the town centre and his statue stands amid the always colourful Kay Gardens.

Bury has also been long famous for black puddings and these must have been good for growing lads because the town produced more than its share of prominent Englishmen. Robert Peel (1788–1850), the grandson of good old "Parsley", had an eminent father whose fortune was built on "Parsleys Pennies". Robert was born at Chamber Hall, Bury and eventually became Prime Minister — not just any old Prime Minister but a major one if you will pardon the pun! Robert Peel achieved many things and he was instrumental in repealing the Corn Laws, initiating the Roman Catholic Emancipation Act and founding the modern police force. The latter were first known as "Peelers" and a little later as "Bobbies" and it is the latter name which has stuck.

Although not natives of Bury, Bolton, Oldham or Rochdale, we are Lancastrians and still take umbrage when people describe these grand old cotton towns as being part of Greater Manchester. Bury was an important town when Manchester was "nobbut a village". It worked very hard and its "cotton slaves" deserved their annual dip into the Irish Sea.

Oldham

Rugby League has been a religion in the Oldham area since the professional game began in the late 1890s. Watersheddings was Mecca. These lads were tough and some of the junior teams left many a bruise on their opponents as one of us can well remember. Cricket is also popular hereabouts and we were once involved in a game played in the 1950s at Whitehaven in Cumbria where a professional called Lawson was destroying our confidence. His pretty blond wife was taking a rest from her heavy acting schedule. She was an Oldham lass and her name was Dora Bryan.

Bolton and Oldham were closely associated with cotton spinning but they seem to have worked out a division of labour almost unconsciously. Bolton specialised in fine count spinning whilst from the 1890s Oldham concentrated on spinning coarse cotton, but some weaving was done especially of fustian, velvet and corduroy. The design of spinning and weaving mills were very different. Spinning machinery was much lighter and could be accommodated on several floors but the looms in a weaving shed were much heavier and the building had to be much more robust. The machinery was housed on ground floors and glass skylights were a feature to enable the weavers to have more 'natural' light available. Some towns like Bolton and Oldham tended to specialise in spinning whilst others, like Blackburn and Burnley, concentrated more on weaving.

The word 'mill' is interesting because the first textile factories were driven by rivers and the term watermill was later renamed a textile mill but later operated by steam. This gradual transition can be seen graphically at the Helmshore Textile Mills Museum.

There are written records of weavers operating in the Oldham area from as early as 1592 and in the church registers of the seventeenth century there are several entries under Webster from which we get the surname. Other surnames of this period were Dyer, Weaver and Fuller. Spinning was physically much easier and this work was therefore done by women who became known as 'spinsters'. Looms, especially handlooms, were very heavy and this was work which only strong fit men could keep up with.

Oldham was quick to embrace the Industrial Revolution and by 1845 there were more than 200 cotton mills in full flow employing almost 16,000 people, and in 1866 the population exceeded 80,000. It has been calculated that more than three-million spindles were clattering away, and much brass and a lot of muck and pollution was being produced.

Mill workers needed fresh air and they found it both close to home and by making full use of their Wakes holidays.

Ramsbottom and Rawtenstall

Some of the atmosphere of the old wakes can be seen by taking a nostalgic trip along the East Lancashire Steam Railway which links Rawtenstall and Bury via Ramsbottom.

Ramsbottom was the base for the mill owners the Brothers Grant who were so well known to Charles Dickens that he used them as a model for the portrayal of the Cheeryble Brothers in his novel *Nicholas Nickleby.*

Close by is the mill museum complex at Helmshore which contains photographs, notices, machinery and other artefacts which would be familiar to wakes workers. The mills are almost opposite the head offices of the Airtours Holiday Company, which has continued the tourism boom but shifted its focus to package holidays in search of the sun. The modern generation will certainly get a similar longing for memories of the Spanish Costas when their carefree youth is spent.

At one time the Grant brothers' good deeds were celebrated by the construction of a tower on a range of hills delightfully called "Top o' th' Roof". Around 1900 the tower was at its most popular and crowds gathered on summer Sundays to look down at the Irwell valley and the forest of chimneys which for the rest of the week poked soot into the air. This was almost, but not quite, as bracing as the sea air of the wakes resorts. Sadly, Grants Tower was allowed to fall into dereliction but near Holcombe is a similar structure which was erected to the memory of Sir Robert Peel and which still stands. The view down into the valley now looks beautiful as the Clean Air Acts have so obviously worked, but the decline of the cotton industry has also had its effect.

Rawtenstall takes its name from the Anglo-Saxon meaning a roaring stream and it certainly roared to good effect in the days when the textile mills were powered by water.

The villages hereabouts have splendid names such as Constablelee which denotes the one time presence of a Constable whose job it was to govern the Forest of Rossendale. Crawshawbooth (*shaw* meant a wood and *booth* an enclosure for keeping cattle) is said to have been the site of the last wild-boar hunt to be held in England. The death of the beast meant that the last wild pig from England had gone and Swinshaw Hall, now a retirement home, is said to stand on the site.

If you stroll about these villages, which are now all but joined together into the town of Rawtenstall, it is possible to discover the ancient tracks, bridges and the handloom weavers' cottages. These are reminders of the days before the Industrial Revolution when pollution was unheard of. Textiles was then an environmentally friendly occupation, wakes holidays meant that somebody had 'deed' or the rushbearing was over and there was no need to visit a seaside resort in order to inhale fresh air!

Rochdale

Our introduction to Rochdale began in the late 1950s during a back-packing holiday to Italy, during which we took the ferry to the Island of Capri in the Bay of Naples.

As we were gasping at the beauty of the scenery we joked about it being "nowt like Blackpool." "Aye tha's reet," replied an elegant lady. This was our introduction to Gracie Fields, the Rochdale lass made good and who had a home on Capri. We met her on several subsequent occasions and watched her switch on the Blackpool illuminations in 1964.

Her friendly greeting always meant that Rochdale had a place in our hearts and our friendship with Richard Catlow, the editor of the Observer Group of newspapers in the town, has kept our interest alive.

The town developed alongside the once crystal clear river Roch which is a substantial tributary of the Irwell, and during the period between 1904 and 1925 the whole of its course through the town became culverted.

The textile traditions of Rochdale began with the wool workers in Tudor times, but during the early years of the Industrial Revolution the town made a fortune from cotton. The wealthy merchants soon evolved a civic pride culminating in the building of one of the most elegant town halls in Europe which was completed in 1866. The foundation stone was laid by the Quaker, John Bright who was the local MP and along with Richard Cobden and, of course, Robert Peel, was responsible for the repeal of the Corn Laws and other good works.

The repeal of the Corn Laws meant cheaper food for the working man, and on Toad Lane the locals soon began to set an example by setting up the Co-operative Movement now celebrated by a museum on the original site. "The Pioneer Stores" gained momentum in 1844 following the hardship faced by the mill workers during a series of strikes. The idea was to sell food at competitive prices and to give dividends to those who spent most. The 'divi' became a national institution for more than a century.

Rochdale in the 1880s must have been a fascinating place with hard but co-operative work, civic pride and apart from the Wakes Seaside Resorts Rochdale also had its very own "Weavers Seaport" at nearby Hollingworth Lake.

There is now a well appointed visitors' centre with toilets, book shop, café and Information Centre. There are good facilities for children and for the disabled. A wheelchair is available for hire at the centre.

Hollingworth is not a lake but a compensation reservoir of 120 acres (58 hectares) originally constructed to supply the Rochdale Canal with water.

Gracie Fields switching on the Blackpool illuminations in 1964.

This opened in 1804 and linked Sowerby Bridge with Manchester. At the present time the lake still supplies the surrounding area of canal with up to two million gallons a day, in addition to its central role within the Country Park. The stretch of water was, however, well used by the hard working mill hands in Victorian times who used it as a "lung" situated high above the then very grimy towns of Rochdale and Littleborough.

The Country Park was opened in 1974 and since that time has gone from strength to strength. The visitors' centre features an excellent taped slide show giving details of the history and natural history of the area, but anyone with a couple of hours to spare will find the circular Nature Trail a real treat.

From the area of Hollingworth, the bulk of Blackstone Edge can be seen rising to a height of around 1,550 feet (472 metres) above sea level, over which runs a Roman road, much of it still in an excellent state of repair. Close to the lake is the Fish Inn and by the lake are several marshy areas in which grows water mint, yellow iris, water forget-me-not and ragged robin.

The footpath follows the line of an old road, and approaches a one-time toll gate close to which is a metal sign which has been restored and provides a feeling of history which is added to as you approach the hamlet of Hollingworth Fold, which must have been even more isolated before the reservoir was built. It was formerly a weaving hamlet and in the nineteenth century it had a workhouse, a small school and its own public house called the Mermaid. Perhaps it was anticipating the coming of the Lake!

The trail then reaches an area known as the promontory which in Victorian times was known as "Weavers' Seaport"; this should not be thought of as a derogatory title, and when viewed in May and June with rhododendron at its best it is really beautiful. The Victorians certainly knew how to enjoy themselves and a paddle steamer which operated on the lake was often full to overflowing during the warmer months. Fortunately we can still enjoy a short trip on the 'Lady Alice' which is a small motor cruiser.

Rochdale did not only have its own inland resort but was also instrumental in starting the seaside trend, at least so far as Blackpool was concerned. The Taylor family were doctors who established a surgery in their home village of Whitworth. They also became famous in the 1780s as advocates of sea bathing and encouraged visitors to drink many gallons of water to purge them of 'inflammations of the bowel'. The "Whitworth doctors" may well have cured their patients merely by giving them a rest and a breath of air. Blackpool made them very welcome indeed and has done so ever since.

Wigan

Wigan, although world famous for its Rugby League team, is a town much maligned. It does not deserve to be the butt of music hall comedians, and its history and generations of hard working coal and textiles workers deserves better.

Those in search of 'Wigan and its Wakes' should begin by visiting "The Way we Were" exhibition at Wigan Pier. The town is at the centre of five 'C's. The Roman town was known as Coccium, the Rugby team are the Cherry and Whites and the wealth of Wigan was built upon coal, cotton and the canal. This latter was not only the lifeline of the town but the route taken by the workers to the developing seaside resort of Southport.

"The Way We Were" exhibition deals with all these aspects and the complex is staffed by resident actors and actresses who bring the scenes to life. We have often thought that each resort, especially Blackpool, ought to have a specially designed Wakes Museum. As we shall see later, the Pleasure Beach at Blackpool has its own museum but the whole Wakes theme does need to be celebrated. The only serious effort so far has been made at Wigan and among the displays are Punch and Judy

The Weavers Seaport — Hollingworth Lake, Rochdale, at the turn of the century.

exhibitions and a bathing machine. The exhibition has also been brave enough to celebrate the life of George Formby Senior, a music hall comedian, who first "invented" Wigan Pier. Actually, his real name was James Henry Booth and he got his stage name by reading the destination Formby which was written on the side of a loaded coal truck. Wigan had not one but many piers, each being a wharf on the Leeds to Liverpool canal along which coal could be unloaded via a chute and directly into barges.

Wigan lads were quite correctly proud of their heritage and not only did they work hard but they also played hard. Those who came from "Wiggin" spent a lot of their brass on the amenities provided by the resorts of New Brighton and especially Southport, but also Lytham St. Annes, Blackpool, Fleetwood and Morecambe. We know that wages were not high in those days, but you could have a six-day holiday in Blackpool for £1/18s/4d — approximately £1·92!

Let us now move on to explore the north-western seaside resorts and discover where and how the working lads and lasses spent their hard earned brass.

23

CHAPTER TWO:

New Brighton

"Along the shore is a narrow unsafe promenade called Aquarium Parade but perhaps better known as 'Ham and Egg Terrace', the favourite resort of the Liverpool and Lancashire trippers and roughs... with more visitors and fewer trippers New Brighton would be flourishing."

This extract from the writings of Sulley in 1889 suggests that New Brighton was the toughest of the north-western resorts and, to be honest, this does seem to have been the case — it was certainly regarded as "even more vulgar" than Blackpool. No-one grieved when this 'den of iniquity' was demolished in 1906 and replaced by the Victoria Gardens with its Floral Pavilion and bandstand.

In 1830 a Liverpool businessman named James Atherton sailed across the estuary bar and looked upon the fine beach and behind it the rolling mass of sand dunes which once, and perhaps still was at that time, the haunt of smugglers. Here at the gateway to the Wirral peninsula one man's dream of building a New Brighton to rival the old watering place down south was born. Atherton bought 170 acres (58 hectares) and set about attracting a few rich people. He also instituted a steam ferry linking his New Brighton to Liverpool. The railway and road links under the river later added to the popularity of New Brighton. What he spawned was a heaving resort catering for large numbers of people given a new freedom by the advent of the railways. We use the word freedom rather

Opposite: *Port Sunlight village, built by William Lever for his workforce.*

loosely because early rail travel involved sticking to the rules. We wonder how the modern 'away day' ticket holder would react if faced with the set of rules given in 1904 to those travelling from Staffordshire on Bass, Ratcliffe and Gretton's Brewery excursion to Liverpool and New Brighton on the Midland and Cheshire railway.

"It is imperative that all persons should travel both ways by their own train. Changing to other trains, and particularly staying for later trains cannot be allowed, as such irregularities upset the arrangements, and seriously interfere with the comfort of the proper occupants of such Trains. All persons detected breaking this urgent regulation will be left behind at Burton or Liverpool, as the case may be, and the *Excursion Ticket will be forfeited*. By the number on the Ticket I can tell conclusively to what Department and Train the holder belongs. It must be distinctly understood that I will not deliberately disregard this most important instruction. We have, hitherto, had no difficulty at Liverpool, but a word of warning may not be out of season, having in mind the trouble I had at Blackpool in 1900. As everyone always gets off comfortably in the morning, it stands to common sense that the same accommodation will even more comfortably bring you home at night, as a large number stay over for a few days. Be very particular, therefore, in future, to carefully study the Trains Sheet, and travel by your OWN Train, both ways. To say the least of it, those persons who deliberately miss the earlier trains coming home are most inconsiderate of other people's comfort, and I hope this is the last time that I shall have to refer to this annoying disregard of the arrangements."

New Brighton, when reached via the ferry from Liverpool, was unique in the sense that even day passengers felt as if they have been on a holiday cruise and, although the ferry service ceased to operate from 1973, a maritime atmosphere remains; however, the resort has gone through a lean time in recent years.

Many of its features, including the impressive tower and the pier, have gone but in its time the former was as impressive as its rival at Blackpool. Originally planned in 1897 and opened in 1900 the 621 foot (189 metre) tower was 103 feet (31 metres) higher than Blackpool's but was sadly neglected during World War I when the Liverpool area had more important things to worry about, and the tower was demolished in 1921. The theatre and ballroom continued to operate until 1961 when they were destroyed by fire. The visitor of 1904, however, must have been astounded at what New Brighton, with its spanking new tower, had to offer. The view from the top of the tower provided views over the Mersey estuary filled with huge ships, and especially the passenger liners easing their way into the port of Liverpool. There was also a fine view down to the river Dee and behind it the backdrop of the Welsh Mountains.

The tower itself was not the only attraction. The theatre beneath had one of the largest stages in Britain measuring 72 feet by 45 feet (22 by 14 metres), and there was comfortable seating for 3,000 people. There was also a huge dance floor which, it was boasted, could absorb 1,000 couples, whilst on a balcony there was seating for observers. The walls were decorated with the coats of arms of northern towns from which the visitors to New Brighton were drawn.

There was also a billiard room and above this was the well named Elevator Hall which had shops selling fancy goods and holiday souvenirs, and what were described as 'amusing automatic contrivancies operted on the insertion of a coin' — obviously an Edwardian term for a one armed bandit!

On one side of this hall was an aviary with a magnificent collection of colourful birds from tropical climes and also what was intriguingly described as a shooting jungle. On the opposite side were huge cages full of monkeys guaranteed to amuse the visitor, although today we cannot help wondering what sort of life it must have been for the monkeys.

The interest in foreign animals and places was also reflected in the design of the 35 acres (14 hectares) of well kept gardens which surrounded the Tower. A disused quarry was skilfully landscaped to provide a fountain and a pond, all edged with succulent growths of ferns which were very popular in Victorian households. Ferns could be purchased in sealed containers and taken home to be placed in the parlour, which at the turn of the century was a clutter of ornaments of stuffed birds and plants.

Ferns thrived in their container, water evaporating from the layer of soil during the day only to condense on the inside of the glass during the night as the temperature dropped, and thus falling as rain on the ferns. These were known as Wardian cases, designed by a botanist named Ward who collected tropical plants from Mr. Bulley at Ness Gardens on the Wirral. Other features of the gardens were a 'Japanese Cafe', a tree-fringed ornamental lake with 'Venetian gondolas' plying for custom, a 'Himalayan railway' and a water chute plus a menagerie and lion house.

Athletic and cycle tracks plus a well appointed roller skating rink were available to the energetic, while for those not so inclined there were seats. Numerous bars and cloakrooms were provided so that visitors could get rid of their coats in fine weather. The Tower company certainly did its best to see that everything was provided within its grounds, but any seaside resort stands or falls by the quality of its beach and James Atherton's good opinion of New Brighton sand was well founded.

At the turn of the century the sands were clean and hard, a delight for youngsters intending to build sand castles. At New Brighton they had a model to copy in the form of Perch Rock Battery, a red sandstone fort which at that time housed around a hundred soldiers needed to man the eighteen thirty-two-pounder Armstrong guns which guarded the entrance to Liverpool Bay. Built in 1825, the same time as the lighthouse further out to sea, the fort never saw active service except once during World War I when it fired upon either a U-boat or a floating log. The lighthouse was preceeded by Beacon Perch which charged ships approaching Liverpool 6d (2½p) for literally providing the guiding light which was so vital around this notoriously difficult channel.

In 1958, the War Office sold the fort which, after a period as a pleasure centre, has been restored to something of its original condition and there are now exhibitions and a small museum. One thing has remained the same throughout — the wonderful views across the bay.

New Brighton sands were badly affected as Liverpool Docks expanded. The Seaforth complex altered currents and mud, debris and occasionally oil from the docks polluted the beach and this, coupled with the loss of the tower, gradually brought the resort to its knees. Its recovery has been slow but improvements are now being made.

Back in 1904, however, the sands were full of castle builders, donkeys giving rides and, as the sea rolled in, horses pulled the bathing machines into position and guaranteed that modesty would be preserved. Bathing was then a ritual and required a great deal of preparation. Visitors on the Bass, Ratcliffe and Gretton Brewery trip were warned that:

"If you bathe in the early morning take a biscuit and a little tea about an hour before your bath. Never bathe for at least an hour and a half after an ordinary meal, and never until two hours or more after a full meal. It is most important not to go into the water when very hot or very cold. A short walk before the bath, just sufficient to make you warm and not hot, is the best. After your bath a good walk will do you good, and give you an appetite. The whole body should be immersed at once, if possible. The following are signs that sea bathing does not agree with you or that you have stayed too long in the water:– Shivering and blueness of the skin, stiffness in the fingers and chattering of the teeth, giddiness, headache, loss of appetite, and depression of spirits. Dress quickly without dawdling. If you can get a pail of hot water for your feet, as you often can do, it very much promotes circulation, and is a great luxury. All who suffer from their heart, liver, or have internal troubles, can seldom or never take baths in the open sea. Their doctor may, however, prescribe salt water baths at home. Sea bathing is, like many other things, excellent for those it suits, but very detrimental to the health of those with whom it does not agree."

Bathing is now quite dangerous off certain areas of New Brighton but safe locations are marked by flags and there is an efficient beach patrol. Swimmers are catered for by a huge open air pool built in 1934, said to be able to provide space for over 3,000 bathers, and almost four times as many spectators.

New Brighton's pier (built in 1885), for so long the focus of this, as any other seaside resort, was dismantled in 1973 after a hard but unsuccessful struggle by conservationists to preserve it. Taking a realistic view, however, the siltation of the Mersey estuary left the pier looking high, dry and a financial disaster. It may be that it was better to remove it and remember its hey-day; when the retiring rooms were full of folk sheltering from the wind or couples finding a quiet spot for a cuddle in the heat of the day; special smoking rooms were provided and the afternoon pier show was always sold out. An interesting feature in these days of women's liberation was the boast that lavatories were free for women and children.

These days a successful seaside resort must have a good promenade and a variety of places of interest within range of a leisurely car ride. New Brighton's future must therefore be secure since the promenade is magnificent and its headland is the gateway to wonderful Wirral.

There remains some pollution of the Mersey, but this is slowly being addressed and the wildlife of the area is now surprisingly spectacular, especially in winter. Cormorants dive for flat-fish and gulls drop shells onto outcrops of rock to break them and get at the soft nutritious bodies within.

Beyond the swimming pool are coloured rock formations known affectionately as the yellow and red noses. It is said that smugglers' caves once led from these rocks to St. Hilary's Church in Wallasey and Old Mother Redcaps at Egremont. Along the seaweed strewn rocks, waders such as turnstones and purple sandpipers search for crabs and sandhoppers. Curlews wade in the shallow pools and redshanks drag big juicy ragworms from their burrows.

The occasional grey seal may be seen bobbing about on the sea, but the bigger concentrations of this now rare animal are found off Hilbre Island which lies just around the headland of the Wirral and guards the entrance to another once mighty river — the

Dee. Now silted up, the Dee estuary has along its bank a string of fascinating and historic villages including Hoylake, West Kirkby, Gayton (where there is now an RSPB bird reserve), Parkgate and Neston. It was at Parkgate that Handel is said to have put the final touches to his Messiah before setting sail for Dublin where it was performed for the first time. Close to Neston are Ness Gardens which are open to the public and a riot of exotic summer colour but also a joy in winter. Once attached to the home of Arthur Bulley who cultivated exotic plants; his collection now forms the backbone of the Botanic Gardens owned by Liverpool University. These were given in 1949 by Bulley's daughter but with the stipulation that they should be open to the public. There are regular lectures held at Ness, plants are sold and there is a well stocked bookshop.

On the road between these Wirral villages and New Brighton is what is now the Leasowe Castle Hotel. This was built in 1593 by the Earl of Derby (the Derbys were the rulers of the Isle of Man) as a shooting lodge, although the Earl called it his 'New Hall'. In 1634, the Earl bought the fittings and fixtures from the infamous Star Chamber court and brought them back to Leasowe. Before the topography of the bay began to alter there was a racecourse along the sandy dunes, but the track was abandoned and transferred to Newmarket in 1732. Most of the old course is now under the sea, as are a string of once essential lighthouses. Leasowe itself may well have been a bolt hole for the controversial Stanleys in times of civic upheaval.

The castle has served as a house, a secure prison for German prisoners during World War I, a railway workers' convalescent home and has had intermittent periods of serving as a hotel. At the present time, the Leasowe Castle Hotel is ideally situated for those who wish to explore the delights of the Dee and Mersey estuaries and must benefit from a New Brighton revival.

On the Mersey Bank visitors to New Brighton will find much of interest including Birkenhead Priory, Cammel Laird Shipyard, memories of the Mersey ferries, the Eastham Country Park and Port Sunlight.

Birkenhead Priory was founded by the Benedictines in 1150 and it has recently been established as a splendid museum with free admission and open daily with the exception of Mondays. The Chapter House is used for occasional services and wedding ceremonies, and although it was dissolved by Henry VIII in 1537 more of its buildings have survived than has been the case with most of the other abbeys in nothern Britain.

It is possible to climb up to the top of St. Mary's Tower from which there are spectacular views over Merseyside, Wales and, closer at hand, down to Cammell Laird's historic shipyards. This had its origins way back in 1824 as an iron works built by William Laird at Wallasey Pool and where the firms first "iron" ship, which was called the *Wye*, was launched four years later. Charles Cammell, a Sheffield steel producer, did not join forces with the Laird company until 1903.

The Laird family grave can be seen at Birkenhead Priory almost within a stone's throw of the historic Graving Docks where the *Alabama* was built. This was a warship constructed for the Confederate States by Laird who viewed the Southern businessmen as 'pro cotton' and therefore 'pro Lancashire'. The Northern Union won, and although cotton continued to travel across the Atlantic, Laird's support for the South cost him a lot of brass, and the loss of a certain knighthood!

All who are interested in the history of New Brighton and Liverpool must take account of the ferries which only became redundant with the opening of the tunnels. At Woodside the old booking hall of the Birkenhead Ferry has been converted into a café and Visitors' Centre. A ferry, of sorts, still operates but these days it deals more in pleasure rather than providing the essential link between Liverpool and the Wirral. In medieval times the nearest bridge across the Mersey was at Warrington, and therefore ferry crossings were absolutely vital.

Nearby is the Shore Road Pumping Station in which is situated the Giant Grasshopper, a restored and working example of a huge steam pump which removed the water which seeped from the Rail Tunnel below the Mersey.

Whilst most of the Mersey Bank of the Wirral has been swamped by industry, especially oil installations, there remains an area of Eastham Wood which is now designated as a Country Park. This is being integrated into the tourist attractions offered around New Brighton. Another area which should receive more visitors than is often the case is one of our favourite areas — Port Sunlight.

Few men have had such an impact upon world trade as William Hesketh Lever, born in Bolton in 1851. To discover one of Lancashire's favouite, sons we followed in his footsteps along the banks of the Mersey to Port Sunlight and wondered if he ever enjoyed a day at the seaside at New Brighton. No doubt his workers did.

William Hesketh Lever
— a Bolton lad made
good. Seen here in 1901
at the age of fifty.

In 1887, when already a successful soap manufacturer, William, the son of a Bolton grocer, knew that his Warrington based operations could not expand further and what he needed was an area of virgin land which he could design to suit his specific requirements.

The site had to be on the banks of a navigable river so that he could import raw materials, and he also needed a railway line along which he could export the finished product. On an initially wild marshland, which was a haven for wildfowl, he built the village of Port Sunlight which he named after his famous soap. Port Sunlight still has about 900 houses and during their construction more than thirty architects were employed to ensure that no block of cottages looked the same.

Lever looked after his workers better than most of his contemporary industrialists and built a garden village which included a church, a technical institute and a magnificent art gallery which he dedicated to his wife. He introduced welfare schemes, schools with well-qualified staff and a building in which his workers could "engage in genteel entertainment". A cottage hospital was built in 1907 and this continued in use until the National Health Service was started in 1948.

The history of the village can be discovered at the Port Sunlight Heritage Centre, for which a very modest charge is made. Inside is a model of the village, explanations of how the workers lived, worked, played and prayed and there are displays of advertising and soap packaging. It has a collection of more than 6,000 photographs dating from the 1880s onwards and more than 700 advertisments of the period.

We have enjoyed several conversations with Elaine Hazlehurst, one of the public relations officers at Port Sunlight. "We would like to see more visitors from Bolton," she told us, "everybody would love it, especially the children from the schools. William Lever, who eventually became Lord Leverhulme, loved Bolton and if he could have shifted it onto the banks of the Mersey he would have done."

Port Sunlight is now a conservation area and still lies within its original boundaries. Although houses there can now be purchased on the open market, there are strict planning regulations in force. Unilever, the massive industrial network which evolved from the

Bolton lad's enterprise, is still responsible for the maintenance of the environment and landscaping of Port Sunlight.

It is difficult to describe the history of the village within the confines of a page or two, but a few important dates start with the Lever Brothers first factory which began exporting soap on its first day of operations in 1889. Christ Church is the only free church in Britain with a peal of eight bells. Free churches usually only have one bell. It seats 800 and is the biggest church in Merseyside. William Hesketh Lever, the lad who made very good indeed, is buried in the church. Bridge Cottage, which is now the parsonage, was used as one of the sets for the classic film *Chariots of Fire*.

Ringo Starr's first performance with the *Beatles* was in 1962 in the Hulme Hall at Port Sunlight, a fact not often appreciated even by those who study the history of the 'Fab Four'.

Port Sunlight should take an honoured place among the attractions offered by the "New Look" New Brighton. This ensures that each seaside resort in the North West of England has its own unique features and appeal.

New Brighton of the late 1990s has an extensive car park, interpretive signs about the resort and especially Perch Rock, firm flat and much cleaner sand, rock pools, super ice cream and teashops, hotels and amusement arcades. New Brighton may not be New anymore, but it is certainly coming back to life and has regained its self-respect.

CHAPTER THREE:

Southport

There are many old Churchtowns up and down the country, but only one Southport. Old Churchtown is now relegated to a suburb of the mainly Victorian resort, but its genteel atmosphere seems to have influenced the new town rather than being swamped by it, as is the case by many other seaside resorts centred upon old fishing villages. Take your time and explore Churchtown which has a number of lovely thatched cottages, the historic Meols Hall, a church with ancient roots, and magnificently wild and rich sand dunes and marshes.

There was a habitation at Meols from the twelfth century onwards and the hall is open to the public on occasions, but particularly throughout August. Within there are family collections of paintings, glass and china. The present owners are also developing an impressive package suitable for meetings and conferences.

Nearby are the Southport Botanic Gardens set around a boating lake and which has a famous fernery. This no doubt provided the incentive for one of the most famous flower shows in Europe which ensures regular awards in the Britain in Bloom competitions. Within the Botanic Gardens is a museum of Victoriana and a collection of children's dolls. There is also an exhibition of the techniques used by the shrimping industry which once brought fame and fortune to the Southport area. This went on until 1970 when the last horse drawn beam nets were discontinued. Some shrimping is still done from Birkdale

Opposite: *Southport's Seabathing Lake enjoyed record attendances in 1955.*

*The famous Southport
Flower Show.*

Beach using motor traction. There is a delightful little pond and around it is an area where regular performances of brass bands have long been famous. Many of these bands had their origins around the mill towns of Lancashire and Yorkshire.

The Southport Flower Show has been a regular feature during August for more than sixty years. In 1996 a second annual flower festival was established during May which aims to ensure that the mild climate around the town persuades colourful and aromatic flowers and shrubs to bloom throughout the year. Although the show is the highlight of a specific time of the year, the area around Rotten Row is almost always a riot of colour.

In times past the area was a convoluted complex of inlets; sand dunes naturally reclaimed from the sea supported a profusion of colourful native flowers during the summer. The dunes which surround the town today are still a botanist's dream, with rest harrow and sea holly being among the most attractive and interesting species. Rest harrow is a mauve coloured member of the pea family whose roots were once dug up, cut into pieces and shaken with water to produce a pleasant tasting drink known as Spanish Water. This was still being commercially produced when we were children during the 1940s.

The roots of sea holly were also used to titillate the palate, and were once simmered in honey or sugar to produce candies which were called "snow eringoes". These were popular during Elizabethan times and Shakespeare tells us that in *The Merry Wives of Windsor* eringoes were a favourite of Sir John Falstaff.

In recent years the evening primrose, which is the right shade of yellow but not related to the common primrose, has colonised the Southport dunes following its introduction from North America. Some feel that it arrived by accident in the ballast of ships carrying cotton, whilst others think that it was brought over as food, its roots tasting like parsnips which are actually very nutritious. In recent years the evening primrose, whose flowers do actually open at dusk, has been found to be a most useful medicinal plant.

The promenade and gardens during the 1940s.

Extracts from it have been used in the treatment of anorexia nervosa, excessive menstrual blood loss, pre-menstrual tension, migraine, rheumatoid arthritis and multiple sclerosis. The Red Indian tribes of North America used it in the treatment of aching limbs and, significantly, they also administered it to women just after they had given birth.

The Churchtown area is mentioned in the Domesday Book and the Vikings were very familiar with the area. They knew the dune system as South Hawes, North Meols and Birkdale. The latter translates very simply as the valley of the birch trees.

The church is dedicated to St. Cuthbert. This has led some, but not all, historians to suggest that the remains of the saint, who died in AD 687, were carried around Lancashire in the ninth century to keep the holy bones (or more likely its associated treasure) from falling into the hands of the Danes, who had invaded Holy Island in Northumberland. Sacred relics also attracted many pilgrims who paid cash to see them, and hoped the view gave them a miracle cure. Cuthbert's remains made many a long journey before ending up in Durham Cathedral where they now rest in peace.

Twelve such resting places have been listed including Heysham, Lytham, Halsall and Mele or Meols, the latter being eventually renamed Churchtown. There was quite probably a small chapel here long before the Norman Conquest, but the first stone structure is dated to 1128 when King Stephen ruled England. In 1219, St. Cuthbert's Eve was designated a fair day and, as this was in mid-August on the Sunday following 20th August, it became known as "Bathing Sunday".

This tradition meant that folk often travelled long distances in order to "tear off their clothes and frolic in the sea". For centuries the event drew large crowds and as many as 40,000 would arrive by horse and donkey carts as well as on foot. Herbert Collins, writing in the 1940s, remembered a rhyme from his childhood which tells us that:

"At noon behold a band
Of lovely damsels troop along the sand
With eager haste approach the waterside
To give a welcome to the flowing tide —
Clad in flannel dress of blue and red
An oil case cap as covering for their head:
When like the Naiads, as we read at school,
They quick descend and trouble well the pool;
Heedless of being seen by vulgar men,
They dash and splash and dash and splash again."

Sea bathing in these parts thus has a long history, but by the mid-nineteenth century the clergy were condemning the lewdness of events. Certainly the lusty young miners from the Wigan area visiting the new resort were hell bent on having a good time by bathing and eyeing up the wenches. But we move on too quickly!

The church of Meol (or Mele) was given to Evesham Abbey by the Baron of Penwortham and the monks kept control until their abbey was dissolved by Henry VIII. By 1543 John Fleetwood of Penwortham had purchased the living and he allowed it to become an independent parish. During their residency, the monks seemed to have maintained a hospice in the area. This provided a rest and a meal for travellers waiting for the tide to recede and allow them to race across the sands of the Ribble estuary and travel onwards to Lytham and into the Fylde.

At the time of the Civil War of the 1640s the oversands route must have been quite hectic as soldiers rampaged across the battle-scarred country. Prince Rupert's cavalry crossed the estuary following their defeat at Marston Moor near York. Between 1730 and 1739, when things had quietened down a little, St. Cuthbert's church was rebuilt, but its small size indicates that the population at that time was not large. Silting-up of the estuary was already becoming apparent but the local folk still scratched out a living from regular legal fishing, and the occasional wrecking by luring ships carrying valuable cargo onto the many dangerous sandbanks.

Southport promenade and pier entrance, c.1865

This coast is still notoriously difficult to navigate and subject to sudden fogs. On 10th December 1886, the merchant vessel *Mexico* was struck by a storm and hurled high onto the Southport shore, but not before almost the entire crews of the St. Annes and Southport lifeboats had perished in a brave attempt to save her.

A lifeboat station, the first in Britain, was set up in 1776 by Liverpool Town Council. The RNLI was established in 1894 but this station closed during the 1914–18 war and was never replaced. Paul Rooney, the Dune Ranger of Sefton Council, showed us the original site which is close to Formby Point.

The time was soon coming, however, when the area would not lure unwilling mariners from the sea, but welcome eager landlubbers from the grimy mill towns spawned by the Industrial Revolution. Sea bathing was, by this time, becoming increasingly fashionable and the seaside resorts were eager to compete with, and even displace, the "inland spas" where 'taking the waters' had assumed the dimensions of a cult.

Southport's prestigious Lord Street at the beginning of the twentieth century.

The locals of Churchtown already had a history of providing cheap accommodation for the cross-estuary travellers. Wherever there is a demand there will always be some resourceful character eager to make quick money. One such entrepreneur was William Sutton, an innkeeper at Churchtown and known locally as 'the Old Duke'. He transported his customers to the sea bathing machines at South Hawes by horse and cart, a distance of about two miles. There he constructed a rough shelter to protect his customers against the weather and where they could enjoy a 'sand free picnic'. Duke's Folly was initially not accurately named because it proved such a success that towards the end of the eighteenth century Sutton built a permanent structure. This was called the South Port Hotel and the name of the modern resort was used for the first time.

The nearest approach to the actual site of the Duke's Folly lies where Duke Street joins Lord Street at the end of the boulevard. Built into the concrete wall at the end of the gardens are three stone tablets which tell their own story:

> *These tablets formed part of a monument*
> *which stood from 1860–1912 about 24 yards*
> *west of this spot on the site of the Original*
> *Hotel or "Duke's Folly".*
>
> *The Year of our Lord 1797.*

This house was built in memory of
D.W. Sutton of North Meols who was the
First Founder and Executor of South Port,
which was call'd his Folly for many years and
it proved that his foresight was his Wisdom
which should be remembered with gratitude
by the Lords of this manor and the Inhabitants
of this Place also.
This column was erected A.D. 1860 by the
Improvement Commissioners as a tribute of
respect to the late William Sutton, commonly
known as the 'Old Duke', the Founder of
Southport. He was born at Churchtown,
North Meols A.D. 1752, and died there May
22 1840. He erected, almost on this spot
A.D. 1792, the First House in what is now
the flourishing Town of Southport, then a
wilderness of sandhills, the house originally
called 'Duke's Folly' was afterwards known as
the Original Hotel. A Memorial Tablet,
taken from its walls, has been placed on the
NE side of this column, and this street has
received the name of Duke Street in
rememberence of the Old Duke.
Erected in present setting 1928.

Sutton may well then have become too ambitious because in 1803 he was imprisoned in Lancaster Castle for debt. His South Port Hotel, however, was soon surrounded by similar structures as well as cheaper lodging houses built to accommodate the increasing

The post office in London Square, 1902.

stream of visitors flowing in mainly from South West Lancashire and particularly the Wigan area. Southport had an initial advantage over its potential west coast rivals and this was easy transport. In 1774, the Leeds to Liverpool Canal was opened, cutting its branches through the heavily populated mining areas reaching Scarisbrick. Coastal visitors left the canal there and it was a mere four miles to Southport, which was reached by horse and cart. It was a slow but easy route and sailing barges were soon carrying holiday makers eager to replace the coal dust in their lungs with ozone.

It was not just the workers who appreciated the developing resort because wealthy industrialists from Liverpool began to build holiday villas, and by 1812 the baptismal registers were listing Southport rather than South Hawes. Some of these villas still stand and they were close to a tiny stream which was known as the Nile. The flood gates were open and although many still came via the relatively cheap barge, by 1820 there were regular stage coach services operating from both Manchester and Liverpool to the new resort. The coach fare from Manchester was seven shillings (35p) if you travelled inside, but only four shillings (20p) if you were prepared to hang on to the outside. The journey was not so smooth as the canal barge, as the roads of those days were rough and rutted in some places and the stretch between Ormskirk and Southport was composed mainly of soft sand, therefore the going was very difficult.

Nature took a hand in the designing of Southport, as it was, as the Bible tells us, impossible to build on sand, but the area between the two huge dune systems was surprisingly solid. Permission was needed from two Lords of the Manor (Peter Hesketh and Henry Bold-Houghton), whose lands met at this point, and here we have the origins of Lord (formerly Lords) Street. Eventually one side became known as the garden side and the other as the shop side. The shops, however, were never purpose built but developed from householders fitting out their front rooms with counters and shelves. Trade thrived, impressive canopies and arcades were built and salubriously genteel tea rooms evolved.

The pier entrance, 1904.

Some of the arcades became famous meeting points. One of the best at the moment is the beautifully restored Wayfarers Arcade which was built in 1898 and was the work of a Glasgow Iron Foundry. It was restored in the 1980s, its narrow entrance opens out into a surprisingly extensive shopping centre. The elegant boulevards of Southport were visited in 1838 by Louis Napoleon who eventually became Emperor of France. Thus the glorious avenues of France and later Boston, Philadelphia and Washington were modelled on Southport's elegance.

Southport was already booming when the railway came but few tracks can have been constructed more quickly than the links to this resort. This was a sure sign that the highly competitive railway companies were well aware that Southport was quite literally going places. The line from "the sea bathing village of Waterloo" (which almost became an important resort in its own right) was opened in 1848, and this had extended to Liverpool by 1850. By 1855 there was a direct route from Manchester. Southport, at this time, was a much more important resort than Blackpool and had a population of around 16,000 compared to Blackpool's of below 6,000. No doubt because it had no fewer than five railway links, Southport became the third largest seaside resort in Britain after Brighton and Great Yarmouth.

Southport's fairground, c.1910.

The informative Railway Centre on Derby Road is a reminder of these days of steam. Between June and September there are displays of steam and diesel locomotives, steam rollers, buses and a remarkable collection of old photographs. The children's favourite is bound to be Thomas the Tank Engine.

Young and old alike will also be pleasantly surprised by the Zoo and Conservation Trust. The collection of ocelot, lynx, lion, parrot, otter, penguin, reptiles and the Aquarium should not cause any qualms to those who criticise the philosophy of keeping animals in captivity. These days the accent should always be firmly on conservation and, although small, this zoo has the welfare of the individual animals and their preservation very much in mind. Zoos have now gradually managed to combine entertainment with evolution and profit with conservation.

By 18th July, 1846, Southport was important enough to assume its independent administration and under the control of Improvement Commissioners. It set a rate of nine pence (3¾p) in the pound but, following public complaints, this was reduced "for the present" to six pence (2½p).

The new resort began to learn how to sell itself and insisted that:–

> *"The shore at Southport is undoubtedly the*
> *best in the Kingdom; being of gradual*
> *descent for more than a mile before we reach*
> *low water and is free of shoals and*
> *quicksands. Bathing machines, in goodly*
> *order and number, are here employed. They*
> *are upon a new construction, being mounted*
> *on four wheels. On this plan, the danger of*
> *turning the machine in the water is thus*
> *removed — being made to return to the shore*
> *without turning. The owners of the machines*
> *are remarkably attentive and obliging, each*
> *striving to excel in arrangements for those*
> *who are desirous of bathing."*

The rules governing bathing in the nineteenth century were strict, and to our late-twentieth-century eyes both prudish and amusing:

> *First:* There shall be a vacant space of one-hundred yards between the bathing ground appointed for ladies, and that appointed for gentlemen.
>
> *Second:* Any owner of a machine going out of line opposite the front and back posts to be fined five shillings each time he goes beyond the bounds.
>
> *Third:* Any pleasure boat, or other boat, coming within thirty yards of any machine, out of which

any person or persons are bathing the owner of such boat shall be fined five shillings for each offence.

Fourth: If any fisherman throws out of his boat any entrails of fish, or leaves them on the shore without burying them in sand, to be fined five shillings for each offence.

Fifth: Any person or persons undressing on the beach, or in the hills or crossing the shore naked, within one-hundred yards from the two outside posts will be dealt with as the law directs for the punishment of such offences.

Sixth: No person or persons on the charity will be allowed to bathe anywhere betwixt the two outside posts on pain of being dismissed.

Seventh: If any owner of a machine takes any person or persons on the charity within the two outside posts to bathe he will be fined five shillings for every offence.

Signed ....

"Richard Rimmer, pilot, and Richard Ball who are appointed to see that the above rules and regulations are put in force, and to receive the fines. By order of the Lords of the Manor. John Linaker and Samuel Maddock are the appointed Stewards."

The holiday town was now flexing its muscles, and by the time Southport became a Borough in 1867 it already had street lighting in the form of thirty-four naptha lamps, and hackney carriages ferried visitors from the station to the increasing number of hotels and lodging houses. The council was well aware that bored or dissatisfied visitors do not return, and the value of good and varied entertainments plus appropriate advertising was quickly realised.

The entertainment provided has never been as 'vulgar' as, say, on Blackpool's Golden Mile but "good turns" were always a feature of Southport. In 1858, for example, Mr Barnum brought General Tom Thumb to Southport as well as the evocatively named Samuel Lover, who was re-booked following his long show called *An Irish Evening* (with its even longer alternative title of *Paddy by Land and Sea illustrating the national characteristics, legends, superstitions, mirth and melody of his country*).

There were, however, plenty of fairground entertainments including Maxims Flying Machine built in 1906, a wooden roller-coaster, helter-skelter, whip, and a more gentle ride known as a cake walk. At Tom's Tea House, near the pier, a troop of aquatic acrobats led by Professors Osborne and Powsley defied death by diving into barrels and leaping from springboards whilst on bicycles and into frighteningly small areas of water. In the 1930s Pleasureland was very popular indeed.

Southport in modern times is fast developing as an impressive conference centre but even this has a long pedigree. In 1860 more than 200 clergymen held an evangelical conference in the Town Hall and this proved to be so successful that it became an annual event for many years.

The new town council soon saw the need (and the potential profits) of a centrally situated purpose-built conference hall which could double as an entertainment centre. The foundation stone was laid in 1871 by Princess Mary of Cambridge and Cambridge Hall opened its doors in 1874.

Its success set the wheels of private enterprise turning quickly and the Winter Gardens began to take shape at the end of Lord Street. Planned to look like a huge conservatory of the "Crystal Palace" type, it had a covered promenade as protection from the rain, leading into a pavilion where a forty-piece orchestra serenaded the customers. The initial cost was a then staggering £90,000 and therefore no space could afford to be wasted.

Beneath the promenade was an aquarium, then very much of an experiment, and by the turn of the century there was also a zoo, dance hall, roller skating rink, music hall, theatre and what were termed 'displays of animated pictures'. All of these joys could be sampled for an inclusive cost of 6d (2½p), but money was always hard to come by.

Despite all the planning the profit margins produced by the Winter Garden's complex proved too small and it was quite sick at the onset of World War I. It did not finally die until the last building of the complex was demolished in the 1960s.

Southport's gardens have long been its joy, and the flower festival still maintains this colourful tradition. Its misery has been the ever receding sea, which is becoming more elusive as the mouth of the Ribble estuary silts up. It has never, however, been as dry as some critics suggest, so Southport-by-the-Sea is still a viable description and one which its local council sensibly takes care to protect.

The speculators had an answer to the retreating water and that was to follow it! What was needed was a long pier, and in 1859 a company was formed and engaged Brunlees from London to design a structure, which was built by W. and J. Galloway of Manchester. The contract was completed within a year and the 1,200-yard pier was opened in August 1860, the first of its type to be built in Britain. Instead of marvelling at the feat, folk complained that it was too long to walk to the end and a railway had to be built down the

Southport beach seen in the 1920s.

centre. During the course of its history the pier railway has had several forms of traction, including the first which was just a strong man pushing a trolley as if his life depended upon it! In 1865 came the first cable car in the world, which was operating eight years before that of San Francisco's. Then came electric and now diesel traction. From 1953 to 1973 we remember the wonderful *Silver Bell* which chugged along for a slow but glorious five minutes to the pier end.

From the end of the pier steamers carried passengers to and from North Wales, the Isle of Man, Barrow and other west coast ports. Still the sea retreated and by 1868 the pier had been extended to 1,460 yards, but the battle was eventually lost and by the 1920s the large vessels could no longer tie up so this aspect of Southport's history was at an end. The last steamer chugged away in 1924 and the pier is now mainly used as a prominent angling and birdwatching platform.

Arguably, the pier's greatest moment in world history came in 1927 when it was in direct line with the solar eclipse and the world's foremost astronomers gathered to use it as a viewing platform. Until Southend's pier was built in 1897, Southport's was the longest such structure in Britain. A fire in 1933 caused considerable damage and by 1936 it had been purchased and refurbished by the local authority. Another fire, in 1959, resulted in major repairs and a reduction in length to 1,211 yards, but its future is now safe as the pier is now a listed building.

In late July an ambitious Pier Festival is held and apart from open air and almost impromptu entertainment there is a theatre, concerts suitable for all tastes and a variety of sporting events. Look out also for the traditional Punch and Judy show and the spectacular fireworks displays.

The business brains of Southport having failed to beat the sea, decided to join it by constructing a magnificent 86 acre (345 hectare) marine lake which, unlike the tide, never went out. Illuminated in summer, it forms a magnificent attraction and a pleasant promenade allows visitors to stroll around it. In winter the wildfowl are a delight to birdwatchers, whilst boaters and windsurfers always seem well able to live in harmony with the wildlife. In summer it is possible to enjoy a quiet cruise around the lake on the *Mississippi Queen*, a comfortable little paddle steamer.

In August 1931, a wooden footbridge was opened to connect the new Sea Bathing Lake with the Marine Lake. This had a strong Lancashire Wakes connection as the bridge was officially opened by Louise Heath of Tyldesley, near Wigan, who was the Lancashire Cotton Queen of the year. A fashion parade was held to celebrate "The Lancashire Cotton Fabrics Fair". Present among the finalists were the beauties of Miss Burnley, Accrington, Wigan, Chorley, Blackburn and Rochdale, but Louise Heath held them all off to take the title!

The Reverend Charles Hesketh gave to the town an area of land which had been naturally reclaimed from the sea and this was converted into a park designed by no less a personage that Paxton. Botanical gardens were opened in 1875 and golf links sprang up and began the long association between the town and professional golf. By the 1930s there were seven well patronised links and Birkdale was already world famous. These days there are nearby courses at West Lancashire, Formby, Hillside Southport and Ainsdale, Hesketh and a municipal course. The pride goes to Royal Birkdale which is planning the 1998 British Open Championship.

Sefton Council has recently published an informative booklet entitled *Walks on the Sefton Coast*. It consists of maps of a very high standard plus illustrations and text which cover the area between Liverpool and Southport.

Don't be fooled by thinking that Merseyside and the Lancashire coast is all litter, industry, muck and pollution. It is actually none of these things and the sand dunes in the area are the finest and most extensive to be found in Britain.

Some years ago local councils were not famous for their conservation work but things have changed during the 1990s. Great strides have been made recently to protect two of Britain's rarest animals — the natterjack toad and the sand lizard. Local authorities desire praise when they have spent money and man power for the good of wildlife and the environment.

From the car park at Formby we followed the footpath through the dunes towards the sea. Although it was winter and a biting wind swept through the area we were able to find the damp area where the natterjacks and the sand lizards hibernate. There was much to see as huge flocks of birds swept in from the sea. We were standing near the site of the first purpose built lighthouse station in Britain and it was here that we found Paul Rooney, the Ranger in charge of this stretch of coast. Paul is not "the Lone Ranger" as he is helped by a number of equally dedicated staff.

Paul showed us how sand dunes were formed by a combination of sand, wind and pioneer plants such as marram grass which traps the sand in its roots and leaves. The sand is piled up into "mini-dunes" which get gradually larger and more stable. It may take a hundred years or more for a dune to mature and because there are too few left these days they have to be protected. The coastal scenery is so attractive that speculators would love to build even more golf courses and houses on the stable dunes. This is no longer possible around Sefton as all the land is now council owned and their attitude is now very much a case of "hands off".

As we walked the dunes and looked out to sea our winter birdwatch became ever more impressive, and our species list included oyster catcher, dunlin, sanderling, shelduck, scaup, wigeon, stonechat, meadow pipit, skylark, kestrel and a flock of more than 200 pink-footed geese flew off in the direction of Southport.

A feature of Southport in the 1950s was 'The Land of the Little People'. Seen here in 1957, it featured a model railway with a beautiful castle overlooking a lake in the background.

In addition to impressive dunes and magnificent golf courses there is no shortage of good, hard sand. During the '20s and '30s huge crowds gathered to watch motor racing with the distant sea as a magnificent backdrop. Even Sir Donald Campbell raced here. In 1926, Sir Henry Seagrave set up the world landspeed record of 160 mph on Southport's sands.

These days the solid flat sands are an ideal focus for the September Air Show which features parachute displays, trade and military stands, vintage aircraft as well as dramatic fly-pasts including the Red Arrows and vintage World War II aircraft. Model aircraft are also on spectacular view. Aviation history was made here, as in 1911 W.G. Higginbottom delivered forty letters from Birkdale to Southport and initiated the first air mail service. Throughout the 1920s and 1930s "Air Liners" made regular stops at Southport.

Philip King, the present Chief Tourism and Attractions Officer, is fortunately a realist but with more than a touch of optimism. He told of the plans afoot to provide the resort with an improved pier and to propel this major historical structure into and beyond the next century. The pier is now protected by a Trust but under the management of the local authority, and it is to be "upgraded" gradually as and when funds allow. Southport is historically the most important pier in Britain and it would seem to be a candidate for a substantial slab of National Lottery of Millennium money!

It is planned to replace the railway along the pier with a road, which will also provide tours of the resort. Such schemes have been a wonderful success in France, and Southport has just as much to offer as any French resort with the sole exception of the weather!

Southport, as already mentioned, is too often dubbed the 'seaside town minus the

The marine lake at Southport in the early 1980s.

sea' but those who level this accusation have not been to the resort very often. It must be admitted that silting-up has caused problems, but high tides do lap the promenade and we always regard the hard, clean expanses of beach as a bonus. The water to some eyes looks dirty but Southport, like those of most of the North West coast, has a sandy beach and the particles in suspension look brown. Many continental resorts are rocky and therefore look cleaner but have water much more heavily polluted than that around Southport.

The last word on this resort must concern the sea which, it has to be admitted, is still running away from Southport. There are, however, occasions when a combination of spring tides and stiff breezes drives the waves under the stout legs of the pier and over the promenade, hurling spray into the marine lake and car parks and soaking the plants in the gardens in a mist of brine. These scenes are mainly a feature of winter but way back in 1915 when World War I was at its height, Southport was advertising itself as a "charming winter resort" as well as a fine-weather venue. Nothing has changed; the charming elegance of Lord Street remains and the scent of the sea is still strong and carried on the bracing breezes.

To say that nothing has changed is not quite accurate as, along with many other seaside resorts in Britain, Southport is fighting back in response to adverse criticism generated by public relations officers from Spain who sell very little except sun and cheap drink. The sun will always be there but inflation is now catching up with the Costas and visitors are asking the question — what do we get for our money except sun? The answer is not a lot.

Southport's answer has ever been the gentle exploitation of its amenities, its wonderful coastline and a series of the best golf courses in the world.

The resort is spending £4 million on the construction of a new sea wall, with the funds being supplied by the EEC and the Ministry of Agriculture and Fisheries. The new wall will protect many acres of land for development between the pier, and by the next century will have upgraded attractions which will be the focus for private funding of hotels and conference facilities. The Ocean Plaza complex will cost at least £25 million and may well lead Southport into the Premier League of European seaside resorts during the next century. William Sutton would be proud of the town he founded, and his successors look far less likely to follow his example and allow unwise expenses to exceed Southport's remarkable assets.

CHAPTER FOUR:

Lytham St. Annes

The title of this chapter may please neither the inhabitants of Lytham nor those of St. Annes-on-Sea since the origins of the two are so very different. They now merge so perfectly together, however, that they seem to be one unit until you examine their architecture or delve into their respective histories.

The two joined forces in 1922, no doubt in an effort to hold their own against the increasing prosperity of Blackpool. To begin with, St. Annes preferred to link with Blackpool, but this suggestion was abandoned following a trivial squabble.

Blackpool refused financial support to the ladies' orchestra which played on St. Annes Pier and the locals took umbrage. There was also such rivalry between Lytham and St. Annes that Councillor C.F. Critchley, who was the first Charter Mayor, felt the need to plead with the residents to "Put aside suspicion, for what we do now will affect the welfare of our children and their children." The new coat of arms was prophetic and was "Salus Populi Suprema Lex." It means "The welfare of the people is the highest law." The dust has now settled — almost — but nobody can dispute that Lytham and St. Annes still have separate and distinct histories.

These days the twin towns have absorbed a number of suburbs and the Borough is known as the Fylde, the name being a reminder of the days when the area was a mossland with a number of reclaimed 'fields' or 'fyldes'. Some of the lovely villages embraced by the Fylde are Wrea Green, Freckleton, Warton and Kirkham.

Opposite: *A windmill has stood on the village green for 800 years.*

Lytham is not actually a seaside town at all but is firmly set on the estuary of the river Ribble across from Southport. The silting process has reduced the once wide and, for small boats at least, easily navigable river into a narrow ribbon almost choked by wide expanses of salt marsh.

Lytham merited an important mention in the Domesday Book under the name of Lidum but evidence suggests that it is actually much older than the eleventh century. This theory is supported by the fact that the parish church, like that of Southport on the opposite side of the estuary, is dedicated to St. Cuthbert. Close to the present parish church is a stone cross bearing the inscription "According to ancient tradition, the body of St. Cuthbert about the year 882 AD once rested here."

Obviously this meant that the saint, who died in the seventh century, had been disturbed in order that his relics, which were encrusted with precious jewels, could be preserved. In the early 1900s Canon Hawkins fixed a new cross shaft to mark the spot but the socket is almost certainly original.

In 1199, during the reign of the infamous King John, most knights were a strange combination of ruthless warlords and religious penitents. Perhaps they felt that gifts to religious orders could negate their sins in other directions. Roger Fitz Roger (Fitz meant son of) gave lands and probably a wooden Saxon church to the Benedictine monks of Durham to enable them to establish a cell to the honour of St. Mary and St. Cuthbert.

Lytham Priory was never a large establishment and there were never more than three monks present at any one time, although in their more luxurious days they may well have had a number of servants. They did, however, control a large amount of land and were never slow to resort to litigation should anyone wish to erode either their influence or their income. There were boundary disputes galore and there were even several documented disagreements with the mother house at Durham which eventually led to Lytham Priory governing itself.

The local people seem, on the whole, to have accepted their lot, although the monastic court records do occasionally indicate minor indiscretions. Some apparently helped themselves to a branch or two from the estate's woodlands. The rule was that peasants could cut dead wood or small branches but were never to fell trees. They could take any timber which they could pull "by a hook or by a crook" but they must never wield an axe. Hence we have the phrase "by hook or by crook".

Others were prosecuted for what seems to us to be the minor offence of failing to clean out a ditch. When you consider that the Fylde was low lying but valuable farmland, poor maintenance of a ditch could lead to flooding and the loss of livestock by drowning or the destruction of crops by leaching out the fertility of the soil.

By all accounts, the locals were not averse to stealing cargo from ships beached on the shore or along the estuary and some were also prosecuted for catching fish claimed by the monks, but sold instead at Preston market. Lythamers were usually an honest and hard working lot but as tough as people of the sea had to be. They had, and still have, brine in their veins and deserve to be called "sand grown uns". We've met many of 'em and they are like sand — 'abrasive' until you get to know them and then they are best described as 'gritty'.

The Benedictine Priory stood on the site of the present Lytham Hall until the monks were dispersed in 1539 on the orders of Henry VIII. The land was then leased to Thomas Dannet for the then substantial sum of £48/19s/6d per annum. In 1554, Sir Thomas Holcroft was in possession of Lytham, but in 1597 it passed to Sir Richard Molineux. The 14th February, 1606, was, however, the most important day in the historical calender of Lytham because on this date the manor was purchased by Cuthbert Clifton of Westby for the enormous sum of £4,300.

The Clifton family of Westby had a proud lineage even before their acquisition of Lytham, and were influential in the Fylde from the twelfth century. Their motto "Mortem aut Triumphum" which means "Death or Triumph" suggests that it was the Triumph part of the phrase which was always the most dominant. Their crest shows a raised sword.

Cuthbert Clifton immediately demolished the monastic buildings and constructed an Elizabethan mansion. Even though the hall has since been rebuilt, part of the kitchen still retains the old monastery wall and the so called Monks Walk still exists.

Other features dating to the Elizabethan period are the ice house and a splendid dovecote which had more than 800 nesting spaces. Both these features were essential until the coming of modern methods of preserving food. The ice house is a huge structure almost 40 feet (12 m) high and looking like a fortification lined with brick. This was filled with hay to insulate it and during the winter ice was collected from a nearby pond and packed tightly into the ice house. This ensured a ready supply in all but the hottest of summers.

Dovecotes were a feature of all large medieval establishments and the breeding biology of doves (also called pigeons) ensured a supply of fresh meat throughout the year, especially in winter. Doves, unlike most birds, breed throughout the year and so young birds (called squabs) could be taken and eaten before they flew. The pigeons guaranteed protein whilst among the low lying mosses of the Fylde there would also be large flocks of wintering wildfowl. These could be caught by the use of decoys, all of which have now faded into history, but an example which would once have been typical of the Fylde design can be seen in working order at Abbotsbury in Dorset.

The decoy consists of a huge wide mouthed net which narrows towards the end. Birds move into the mouth of the net attracted by food and are then flushed into the trap by a well trained dog and an equally skillful handler. The monks, and later the Cliftons, would not have been short of fresh meat for the table and they would also have used a falconer as another means of killing birds in the days before accurate firearms were developed.

Cuthbert Clifton mixed with the highest in the land, and he was one who visited the de Houghton family at Hoghton Tower near Preston. He was there on the famous occasion in 1617 when the King enjoyed his meal so much that he knighted a loin of beef and thus created the term Sirloin. Many historians think this is legend but Sir Bernard de Hoghton was kind enough to show us the menu of this fabulous feast, and if the King did not knight something or somebody then he was failing in his duty. Cuthbert Clifton remained with the King as he travelled onwards to Lathom Hall, the home of the Stanley (Lord Derby) family, and here Cuthbert himself was knighted! At Astley Hall in Chorley the actual chair on which James I sat during the Knighting ceremony is on display.

Sir Cuthbert was a fertile man, even by the standards of the time, and he sired seven daughters and six sons but the sons met with considerable trouble during the Civil War. Four were killed between 1642 and 1645 and this caused great sadness to the people of Lytham who apparently held the family in great affection. Fortunately Sir Cuthbert did not have to witness this tragic period as he had died in 1634 and was succeeded by his son Thomas.

The Cliftons supported Charles I against Cromwell and they remained devout followers of the Stuart family. They held to the Stuarts and the Old Religion and they suffered greatly because of this. The event which caused the greatest publicity for the family concerned what became known as "The Lancashire Plot" of 1694. Sir Thomas Clifton may or not have been directly implicated, and despite being imprisoned in the Tower of London he was later acquitted following his trial in Manchester. The chroniclers of the time pointed out that the poor man became so worn out by these events that he died. The Lancashire Plot involved the attempt to restore James II to the throne following the successful rebellion by William of Orange and Queen Mary in 1688.

Sir Thomas's son had already died, which meant that the estate passed to his nephew, who was also called Thomas Clifton. It was his grandson, born in 1727, who built the present Lytham Hall, and he had the good sense to employ one of the best architects of the period who was John Carr of York. He supervised the construction which took place between 1757 and 1764. There must have been considerable pressure on the family to renounce their ties with Catholicism. In 1778, yet another of a long line of Thomas Cliftons did turn Protestant, but this may just have been lip-service because his descendants seemed to revert to the Old Religion as soon as it was prudent to do so.

The Protestant Thomas was a wonderful servant to Lytham and he it was who reclaimed large areas of the Ribble estuary, drained the moss, built a lighthouse, endowed a hospital, planted thousands of trees and established the minor Church of St. Annes which later gave rise to the second half of the name of the modern resort. It was also this Squire Thomas who established Clifton Drive which became the Blackpool boundary with Lytham and hence the name Squires Gate.

Lytham Hall is still a fine example of a Georgian manor house and has been maintained in recent years by the Guardian Royal Exchange Insurance Society. The last Clifton to live in the hall was Mrs Violet Clifton who died in 1961.

In 1800 Lytham was still described as "an obscure place" and in 1813 the "Cursory Description of Lytham" would no doubt have pleased the clergy when they read:

"One circumstance above all must render Lytham dear to those who have a strict regard to morality — vice has not yet erected her standard here. The numerous tribes of gamblers, unhappy profligators and fashionable swindlers find employment and rapine elsewhere. Innocent recreational delights, riding, walking, sailing and other modes of pastime banish cares from the mind, whilst the salubrity of the air expels disease from the body . . . [there are] two most excellent bowling greens on which some part of the company are frequently seen enoying themselves with a revolving bowl."

The "revolving bowl" is still very much with us and has now been joined by the flying ball since the town, rather like its rival Southport, is fringed by a number of good golf courses. These include the world famous links at Royal Lytham and St. Annes which regularly hosts the British Open Championship. The Green Drive is well named for a golf course and Fairhaven is also a taxing and well-maintained course.

The history of golf in the Fylde makes fascinating reading because initial efforts to establish the game were focused on Blackpool but little or no interest was shown by the council at that time. Alexander Doleman, who was the instigator, eventually lost patience with Blackpool and simply walked across the border where he was welcomed with open arms and in 1886 the Lytham and St. Annes Golf Club was founded. Following the successful British Open in 1926, which was won by Bobby Jones, the course was allowed to add the prefix 'Royal'. Tony Jacklin began the revival in British golf by winning the Open at Lytham in 1969.

The Fairhaven Golf Club was established in 1895 with the joint ownership of the Squire and the Fairhaven Estate Company. The course was directly on the seafront, but it soon suffered from inundation by high tides and the original clubhouse was flooded. Later, the headquarters was moved and the original building has become the Fairhaven Lake Cafe.

Fairhaven these days is famous for its lake, sited at the western end of the seafront with its 1·5 mile promenade. Here, wind surfers, yachtsmen, rowing and motor boats, as well as water skiers, have discovered how to live at peace with each other. The birds have also learned to find the sheltered areas, especially during a busy summer. During the hours of darkness, and especially in the winter, the birds often have the lake to themselves. The cold weather bird watcher can study goldeneye and other species of duck, canada geese and both whooper and mute swans roosting on the lake. On the muddy beach on the seaward side of the promenade are masses of waders which find the area ideal for feeding. This stretch is one of the best places in Europe for watching sanderling. This little wader is around eight inches (20 cms) long and its pale body is easily seen against the dark mud and sand. Its habit of feeding by running into the sea like a clockwork toy and grabbing an item of food before scuttling away to avoid being swamped by the next wave is both typical and amusing. The area is supervied by the Royal Society for the Protection of Birds who pay particular attention to young ornithologists. It is always good to see how resorts and conservationists can work together rather than become polarised and often bitter rivals.

There is also excellent bird watching from Lytham Green dominated by the white painted windmill built in 1805 and set amid lush lawns, which were laid out in the 1830s as sea defences and overlooked in one direction by the sea and on another by large houses and the church spire. There have been mills in Lytham from at least 1190, and the present building was obviously ideally situated to pick up the sea breezes. It has not worked since a fire in 1918. In 1929 a strong wind blasted the vanes so fiercely that they rotated in the wrong direction and shattered the mechanism. The old mill is now the focus for a museum where we enjoyed interesting conversations with Doris East a local historian and Frank Kilroy an enthusiast about lifeboats which also feature prominently in the museum. Admission to both the windmill and the lifeboat museum is free and are run by local volunteers who adopt a professional and very proud approach to their heritage.

The history of the local lifeboat has a long and proud tradition. This first Lytham Lifeboat House was constructed in 1851 and cost £298. It continued to operate until 1960 when a new lifeboat station was built, but the old building well deserves its place in

St. Anne's Lifeboat, Laura Janet. This was the vessel lost with all hands who attendeed the Mexico

history. The town had its own independent station until the Royal National Lifeboat Institution was established. This was largely because of the *Mexico* tragedy, which was described in the Southport chapter. An impressive memorial to those who drowned can be seen close to St. Annes Pier, but the area had an earlier tragedy which is less well documented. In 1852, the Yarmouth built lifeboat capsized during a rescue attempt and eight of the crew lost their lives. It was, however, the Southport and St. Annes disaster which brought about serious considerations regarding the design of lifeboats.

Some confusion has been caused as it is not often realised that the Lytham lifeboat, and that of St. Annes, were actually separate institutions although the men all knew each other and were often related. The only way to describe the events is to quote directly from the Coxswain's diary. It was the Lytham crew which originally discovered the tragedy which befell those at Southport and St. Annes.

> *"On Thursday night 9th inst. signals of distress were seen from a vessel to the south Westward. The lifeboat was launched at 10 o'clock and under sail and oars was taken some distance to windward then under oars across the banks over which a fearfully heavy sea was running and when near the distressed vessel which was close to Southport the anchor*

was let go and the lifeboat veered down alongside the ship, the seas here were mountain high and breaking right over the ship which was on her beam ends. The vessel was found to be a barque with only mizzen mast standing and the crew were lashed to rigging. The lifeboat was over and again filled with water and the twelve-man crew of barque were with greatest difficulty picked off the wreck, during this operation four of the lifeboat oars were broken by the seas. Having got the men safely into the lifeboat she was turned about and made for Lytham getting here a little after 3 in the morning.

10th December, 1886: This morning the life-boat was launched to go in search of the St. Anne's lifeboat which had put off the night before to the assistance of the 'Mexico' and had not since been heard of. Fears were entertained that she had met with some accident. These fears were too well founded as soon after the return of the Lytham boat from a further search news was brought that the St. Anne's lifeboat had been found bottom upwards on the shore near Southport and all her crew drowned."

The story of the local lifeboats is graphically told in John Kennedy's book *The Lythamers* which covers the history of the Lytham lifeboat and its crews from 1844 to 1986.

Those who wish to avoid sea breezes will find Lytham St. Annes well supplied with sheltered tree lined walks including the Lowther Gardens off West Beach. The foliage gives each putting course, tennis court and bowling green its own individuality and the flower beds are masterpieces of horticultural planning.

In February 1846, the rail link was completed and day visitors began to arrive, especially on Sundays, when inland church congregations began to decline to such an extent that some preachers called the excursions as "Safe and Swift Trips to Hell".

Would Lytham, everyone wondered, eventually knock down the windmill and lifeboat station and spread concrete to make room for a fun fair? Thanks to the Clifton family this was resisted, prices were higher than at Blackpool and a quiet opulent image was soon established which was firmly underlined as St. Annes-on-Sea was planned. Rich manufacturers from the cotton towns of industrial, and at that time very mucky, Lancashire eyed up the dunes between Lytham and Blackpool and the hard earned brass of King Cotton meant that the days of empty sand were numbered. From 1840 onwards Lytham folk let their hair down and 'Club Day', which still takes place each June, is a spectacular event, but not to be outdone St. Annes holds its carnival in July. The joint town thus enjoys two days of frolic and fun.

St. Annes had to be developed because the river end of Lytham was very much involved in a lucrative industry — ship building. These days we look at the almost deserted creek and imagine that the shipyards were only a minor part of Lytham's history but nothing could be further from the truth. The yard specialised in tugs and 'stern wheelers' which were built with a shallow draft and ideally suited for use on the muddy rivers of Africa. One vessel was named the *Luggard* which became famous as the *African Queen* used in the film starring Humphrey Bogart and Katherine Hepburn. Prestigious orders for the yard included the construction of *The Duke of Brabant* for the King of the Belgians who then owned the Congo. The vessel was built at Lytham and transported in pieces by sea and overland before being reassembled in Africa.

The shipyards worked at full stretch during the First World War and also during World War II when some sections of the Mulberry harbours, which played such a vital role in the Normandy Invasions, were constructed at Lytham. The continued silting of the Ribble estuary and the decline in British shipyards generally led to the Lytham yard agreeing to voluntary liquidation in 1955. The last vessel to be constructed was the Windermere car ferry.

Lytham once had other heavy industries and between 1919 and 1947 the English Electric Company tried hard to establish a tradition of constructing Flying Boats. The main factory was on the site of what is now a bakery, and though it was never successful it did give rise to a multi-million pound project. In 1947, the works was transferred to the

*Lifeboatmen monument
in memory of those men
lost trying to rescue the
crew of the Mexico.*

war time American airbase at Warton, which is now the British Aerospace complex. Just prior to its opening, the M55 motorway was used as a landing strip for a fighter aircraft and this could soon be adapted in the unlikely event of future hostilities.

Running almost side by side with industrial development in Victorian Lytham was tourism, which was developing apace. Like all other resorts the essential requirement was the construction of a pier. The local authority allocated an expenditure of "Six thousand

A Jaguar aircraft on the M55 motorway just before it opened in 1975. It was good publicity, both for the new motorway, and for the British Aircraft Corporation at Warton.

St. Annes pier c.1900.

pounds and no more" and Eugenius Birch built a pier 914 feet (278 metres) in length and the running costs were calculated and could be recovered by charging an entry fee of two pence. Local boatmen engaged upon providing pleasure cruises were able to use the pier on payment of £1 per annum.

Lytham Pier had something of a chequered career, with its heyday being the period following the addition of a Floral Hall complex during the 1890s. Disasters, however, more than balanced the happy events; during a 1903 gale two vessels struck the pier and sliced it in half; the repaired structure was badly damaged by fire in 1927 and as this coincided with the depression of the late 1920s and 1930s — it was never fully rebuilt.

In 1938 the pier was closed but it was not finally demolished until 1960. There can be no doubt, however, that it was the development of St. Annes as an up-market resort which led to the demise of the Lytham half of the eventual partnership.

The "serious" building of impressive mansions began at St. Annes in 1875, but some important lessons were learned from Lytham. Close to the shopping centre are the Ashton Gardens with artificial but very realistic waterfalls hurling a fine spray onto tree lined walks and flower beds.

The name Ashton should be respected in the Lytham St. Annes area, although the great philanthropist lived, and did most of his good works, in the Lancaster and Morecambe areas. James Williamson made his fortune from the production of oilcloth and Lloyd George lifted him to the peerage with the title of Lord Ashton. From 1913 onwards he funded the Alpine Gardens, paid £10,000 for a war memorial in the gardens and gave £25,000 to help in the building of a memorial hospital.

Neither Lytham nor St. Annes were short of influential and wealthy businessmen. The concept of a new town at St. Annes involved the brains of one man and the brass of another, an irresistible combination. Thomas Fair, who is celebrated in the name of Fairhaven Lake, was the agent for the Clifton's Lytham estates and had expressed the opinion that the dunes were ripe for development. The cynic may well point out that this meant that Lytham itself would be cushioned from further exploitation.

In 1874, Elijah Hargreaves, who had made a fortune from cotton, visited the area and he and Fair worked in harness to develop St. Annes which they named after the little chapel built in 1873. Most of the essential finance came from Hargreaves' mill owning friends in the industrial belt around Haslingden and the Rossendale Valley. Red brick villas sprouted quickly from sheltered spots overlooking the beach, which is very safe for bathing and from which the tide receeds a good distance leaving behind hard, clean sand.This has ever since proved ideal for beach sports, especially sand yachting as well as more traditional and less energetic pursuits. Sand yachting is a well-organised sport at Lytham with world championships held here and Paula Leah and her friends take its organisation very seriously indeed.

In time the villas were punctuated by salubrious hotels and the St. Annes-on-Sea Land and Building Company Limited, with the benefit of a 1,100-year lease from the Clifton family, was launched on a very firm footing indeed. Many of the houses had gardens facing the sea an which were decorated with pebbles taken from the beach, thus providing an attractive balance between ancient and modern building materials. Pebbled yards proved very hard wearing in the days when horses were the only means of transport. Many of the buildings were designed by the Bury firm of Maxwell and Tuke.

Another prominent mill owner with an eye on St. Annes was William Porritt also of Helmshore and who used his money to construct houses of stone which he obtained from his own Rossendale quarries. Porritt Houses were typified by being constructed of tough stone but with the end walls of London brick, steeply pitched roofs and terracotta tiles. Many of these still stand and are also recognised by the "Porritt" diamond mark on the green slates. Porritt employed only the best builders and he kept an eagle eye open for those who accepted sub-contract work. Daphne Knapp, who still lives in the area, told us how her grandfather was kept very much on his toes by Mr. Porritt. His stone was also used in the construction of the first town hall and other civic buildings. All the building projects were sufficiently controlled to ensure wide, airy streets and there is no doubt that St. Annes is the best designed of all the north-western resorts.

Initially, St. Annes was physically separated from Lytham but the eventual development of Ansdell between the two effectively sealed the gap. Richard Ansdell was actually a mid-nineteenth century artist who specialised in coastal landscapes and wildlife. He built a house which later became the Starr Hills Methodist Home for the Aged. From 1860 onwards Ansdell became a popular figure and thus the region simply became known as "Ansdell's".

Because so much ill-advised development has been a feature of past Fylde management what does remain needs fierce protection.

Lytham St. Annes Nature Reserve is a wonderful example of good political thinking. It was established in July, 1968, by the Lytham St. Annes Borough Council with help from the Lancashire County Council and the Nature Conservancy Council. There is a

Looking north towards Blackpool from Lytham St. Annes Nature Reserve

well-appointed Information Centre on the site with a warden usually in attendance, but the reserve itself is freely open at all times.

The wildlife here is astoundingly rich with mammals including hedgehog, shrew and short tailed field vole. Breeding birds include linnet, stonechat, skylark and meadow pipit.

It is botanists, however, who are guaranteed the most excitement. On a warm autumn morning we made our way into the reserve which is just opposite the Thursby Nursing Home, which was once a convalescent home for coal miners from Lancashire especially around Burnley. Some of the Wakes workers thus knew the area very well.

Flowers still in bloom included evening primrose, grass of parnasus, sea aster, harebell and sea rocket. It is possible to walk through the reserve, cross the main St. Annes to Blackpool road, and then through another dune system to the sea.

Land around resorts such as Blackpool is always in great demand and we should all give a vote of thanks to the officials way back in 1968 who had the sense to create the Lytham St. Annes Nature Reserve. This is overlooked by Blackpool Airport and the Pleasure Beach but able to live in harmony with it.

Let us hope that those who represent us thirty years on show the same foresight!

As the railways became busier and more efficient it became possible for the mill owners to live by the sea and travel daily to and from the smoky mill towns. It is hard to imagine that the proposal to build a pier would be popular with the rich but eventually an irresistible pressure developed and on the 15th June 1885, St. Anne's Pier was opened.

In its early days the pier was narrow and unpretentious; it was used by pleasure boats which catered for visitors, but wealthy folks were also able to moor their private

Lytham St. Annes Nature Reserve Information Centre

yachts. Victorian and Edwardian England was the heyday of the pier and St. Annes reacted to this by constructing an extension in 1904, and in 1910 the Floral Hall was built. A feature of particular splendour of the 1930s was the Moorish Pavilion which was lavishly coated with gold leaf. It was at the Floral Hall that "lady instrumentalists" led by Miss Kate Earl gave popular musical performances and charged the modest price of one penny.

The pier entertainment was always popular and that at St. Annes has survived for many years despite the ever present threat of storm and fire. In April, 1975, a disastrous fire destroyed most of the pier and the theatre was totally gutted. Unlike many piers, St. Annes decided against demolition and spent money on a restoration and the entrance now looks typically Edwardian in appearance. Long may it remain! The entrance has become a busy amusement arcade. What would Elijah Hargreaves and William Porritt have thought of this?

Other remnants of Edwardian England are seen in the form of a number of bathing huts just to the north of the pier. These are still used by summer swimmers as changing rooms and a place to brew up but, although closed in winter, their walls also offer shelter to bird watchers looking out at the waders which feed on the rich sands. This is one of the best sites in the country for watching bar-tailed godwits and ringed plover. Bar-tailed godwits resemble small curlews but with a straight bill and shorter legs. Curlews measure 22 inches (55 cms) but godwits are 15 inches (38 cms). When they fly, bar-tailed godwits have a prominent white rump and the absence of a wing bar is also a diagnostic feature.

Ringed plovers, known locally as stone runners, measure a mere 8 inches (20 cms), but what they lack in size they more than make up for in character as they scuttle around the strand line and are easily recognised by their prominent, black collar and orange legs. Both these species are common but rarities do occur on this coast, and snow buntings seem to find St. Annes, beach much to their liking during the feezing cold days of winter.

Winter is an ideal time for beach combing, as high tides throw fascinating sea creatures up onto the strand line. A collection of shells is easily made and is even more attractive than in the summer because the colours are not bleached by the long hot days of sunshine. Seashore molluscs fall into two classes. The bivalves including cockles, mussels and tellins are so named because their shells are in two halves and hinged in the middle. They lie buried in the sand until the tide comes in when they put out two tubes called siphons. The inhalent siphon draws in a current of water from which food is filtered and oxygen is extracted for respiration. The carbon dioxide and waste matter is eliminated through the shell, which is wound round a spiral column called the columella.

Examples of marine univalves are whelks, spire shells and the delightfully sculptured pelican's foot, so named because it has a twisted structure near the shell entrance which resembles the webbed foot of a bird. Other fascinating natural objects deposited on the beach include the egg cases of dogfish and skate which are both members of the shark family, whilst thousands of tiny cases belonging to a worm — well named the sand mason — are also a feature of many north-western beaches.

Molluscs live well in sand and mud which also protects the empty shells when the animals die. The presence of such vast numbers of shells means that pollution levels along the Fylde coast are not so high as many think. The Fylde beaches have had their critics in recent years but they are a naturalist's paradise and as the water treatment works take effect in the late 1990s things are likely to improve even more.

Fairhaven lake in the winter of 1993 — a birdwatcher's paradise in the colder months

CHAPTER FIVE:

Blackpool

Despite its reputation for brash entertainments and boisterous humour, Blackpool's origins are even more humble than many seaside resorts, with a few entrepreneurs risking all for a modest return. How many visitors have rattled along in a Blackpool tram which runs along the promenade on its way to Fleetwood — a distance of seven miles — and alighted at Uncle Tom's Cabin only to wonder just where it has gone? Writing his *Lancashire Stories* in 1911, Frank Hird provides us with a beautifully written and very nostalgic explanation:

> *"Some thirty or forty years ago 'Uncle Tom's Cabin'*
> *was one of the chief attractions and places of*
> *amusement at Blackpool; now it is only a memory.*
> *Originally it was a little wooden hut, built by a man*
> *called Thomas Parkinson, but who always went by the*
> *name of Uncle Tom. Thus the hut became known as*
> *Uncle Tom's Cabin. Here, in the summer-time, he sold*
> *sweetmeats and ginger-beer to the visitors who had*
> *climbed to the top of the promontory, some hundred*
> *feet above the sea, upon which it stood. Then, there*
> *were nearly a hundred yards of sward between the hut*

Opposite: *Whether it be 1900, 1960, 1980, 1990 (as in this photograph) or 2000, Blackpool will be sure to lead the country in providing the spectacular.*

and the edge of the cliffs. As time went on, it became more and more popular as a resort for Blackpool visitors. They were not so numerous nor so exacting in their requirements in those days. After a while there was a change of ownership; a man called Taylor buying Uncle Tom out for £5. Mr. Taylor was an enterprising person who saw the possibility of increasing the popularity of the little place. He therefore took in a partner, but although the field in which the hut stood, together with an adjoining one, were offered to them for £15 they declined because of the high price! That was fifty years ago; one wonders what the value of the land is today. By a curious coincidence, very shortly after the two partners commenced business, the bust of a negro was washed upon the sea shore, probably the figure-head of a ship, and seeing its appropriateness to the name of their hut, they stuck it up on the roof and added rudely-carved figures of characters in Mrs. Beecher Stowe's novel, "Uncle Tom's Cabin", which was then being sold by the thousand. Thus, they very cleverly seized upon the popularity of the book by giving the impression that their humble place of refreshment was named after its principal hero.

Each year saw the expansion of the wooden cabin, new rooms being added to meet the growing requirements of the visitors. All through the summer there was dancing on the green in front of the building, first to a small orchestra consisting of a pianist, a cornet player and a violinist; then boards were laid down on the grass, as the numbers of dancers increased, and with that increase the orchestra was augmented. In the sixties and seventies of the last century Uncle Tom's Cabin was in the heyday of its success, but with the establishment of the Winter Gardens there came a change. Visitors to Blackpool turned from the humble dancing floor upon which the figures on the roof smiled woodenly, to the veritable palaces erected for their pleasure. So Uncle Tom's Cabin gradually became a memory of the past. A tramway passed close by, but it brought only elderly folk who had known the delights of the place in their youth, and loved to return, and sit for awhile on the grass outside the curious conglomeration of old buildings. Nature completed what the change in fashion had begun. In the last ten years of the nineteenth century no less than forty yards of the cliff had been washed away by the action of the tides and wind and rain. In June, 1901, there was a heavy landslip which threatened the very foundations of the Cabin and the place that had once given pleasure and delight to thousands became a menace to the safety of the public. It was necessary, therefore, to level it to the ground. But so long as it stood it served as an example of the pleasures of the earlier day of Blackpool, a striking contrast with the magnificent halls and buildings Blackpool has erected for the amusement of her visitors today."

We remember speaking to one of our grandmothers, who was over ninety, in 1947. She told us of her memories of Uncle Tom's Cabin but she had enough sense to realise that things always seem more fun when you are young. Uncle Tom's Cabin will never be forgotten because it will always be a tram stop and the name of a modern and popular Public House. Nostalgia should always be an integral part of a resort which is long on entertainment but somewhat short on history.

There were a few historic buildings in the area including the aptly named Fox Hall. Although, like Uncle Toms, the original building has long been demolished its name lives on as a Public House on the Central area of the Promenade.

Fox Hall was originally built as a summer residence by Edward Tyldesley whose main estate was at Myerscough Lodge near Garstang. The family, like many on the Fylde, were staunch Roman Catholics and Fox Hall may well have been a pleasant retreat for them in times of trouble. It was thatched and had several priest holes, stables, a fishpond and gardens of fruit, vegetables and herbs. It may or may not be true that the residence got its name because a tame fox was tethered outside, but this has led to the erroneous assumption that it was the family hunting lodge. It was much more salubrious than that, and was probably the first ever example of the area being used for a breath of seaside air.

In the early eighteenth century most of the Fylde coast was a massive bog with an extensive peaty inland lake called Marton Mere, which is now situated off the main road into the town and surrounded by caravans but threatened by the development of a new football stadium and an associated development. It is a haven for bird watchers in winter when wildfowl are abundant. Its brown waters once fed a watermill and then on to the sea through a creek and thus created a black pool from which the resort took its name. The pool was part of Layton Manor and in the parish of Bispham.

William Hutton, a traveller from Birmingham, described Blackpool in 1789 as a sea bathing resort, although even by 1850 the settlement was little more than a single row of houses. The coming of the railway in 1846, coupled with Uncle Tom's Cabin, proved to be an irresistible recipe. Initially, the railway only went as far as Poulton-le-Fylde with the rest of the trip being completed by horse and trap, but the era of the day-tripper had dawned.

*Bathing machines near
Blackpool's Metropole hotel*

The construction of the Central and North piers during the 1860s provided the icing on the cake and Blackpool, to quote yet another modern cliché, was ready for 'lift off'. When the Winter Gardens was completed in 1876 the flood of visitors became a torrent.

To prevent equally ambitious resorts from competing, Blackpool needed a novelty on which to focus and market its assets. In 1894 the Tower was built, reaching a height of 518 feet (158 metres) and until the London Post Office Tower was built it was the highest building in Britain. There were other resorts such as New Brighton and Morecambe which constructed rival towers but Blackpool's was the only one to survive. It was, however, still only around half the height of the Eiffel Tower on which it was modelled. Its massive

During its construction in 1894, the tower used 5,000,000 bricks, 2,500 tons of steel and 93 tons of cast iron. It cost £235,235 — a small sum these days, but an enormous amount then.

legs straddle a ballroom, bars, restaurants and it also had an Education Heritage Museum. This came too late to educate Stanley Holloway's young Albert Ramsbottom, who visited the mythical lion called Wallace at the zoo, interfered with him using a stick with a horse's head handle and got 'et'.

These days the zoo has been transferred to a magnificent new site beyond Stanley Park and is rapidly establishing a reputation for the animals which it keeps.

In the days before television brought pictures of animals in the wild into our sitting rooms, a visit to a zoo was the only way to see lions, tigers and other magnificent species.

Blackpool Zoo was relocated in 1972 on the site of what was a municipal airport from 1931 to 1946. The zoo offices were once the control centre of the airport and the old hangers are now used as the living area of a giraffe and the Indian elephants. This is the species with small ears, whilst the African species is typical of Dumbo, with huge ears.

The zoo has always provided a good service for schools and there is a classroom which can be used by visiting groups.

We visited the zoo several times during the 1980s and could easily see why conservation and animal-welfare groups were worried. Some animals were kept in very poor conditions and few, if any, scientific studies were being carried out. The curator of the 1990s is Stephen Standley and he is busy restoring the zoo's reputation and establishing a proper breeding programme for several endangered species and improving the living conditions of all the animals.

It is thought that the single giraffe needs a mate, and the Indian elephants who live next door are short of space. The answer is to send the giraffe to another zoo which already has a suitable mate and to give the extra space to the elephants. The elephants will soon be provided with a pool and a "forest" of trees to provide a natural environment.

The breeding programmes, with all records kept carefully on computer, are beginning to work. In 1994 a delightful ocelot kitten was born, and other equally fascinating breeding programmes are in hand.

However well a zoo is run there will always be some people who will want to close it down. We are sure that bad zoos should be shut, but it is essential to keep those which do vital conservation work open and well funded. Blackpool is improving all the time and now has links with zoos all over the world. The combined studies of all these zoos is bound to help scientists keep rare species alive and then return them to their natural habitats.

In the near future Blackpool Zoo will be an exciting place to visit. The large apes, including the gorillas, will have much better living conditions. Ring tailed lemurs will be studied in detail and their cages improved. Blackpool's zoo will therefore continue to be an asset to the resort, as will the nearby Stanley Park.

These days people are conceited enough to think that we invented the terms 'conservation' and a 'multi-purpose environment'. Stanley Park is a perfect example to prove that this was a much earlier concept. Should we consider it as just a park or should the naturalists of Lancashire in general, and the Fylde in particular, list it among the places to watch birds? In our view, Stanley Park is very much a place for the serious birdwatcher mainly, but not exclusively, during the period from October to the end of April.

The Park opened on 2nd October 1926, following a detailed period of planning and with all the associated political posturing. The draft plan of around 1924 reads very much like an ambitious millenium equivalent and took into account the needs of all and, by inference, that of the wildlife as well. Stanley Park was to incorporate an Italian Garden and Social Centre with a restaurant, a bandstand with seating for 2,500 and an eighteen-hole golf course with its club house dovetailed into one wing of the restaurant. There was to be a twenty-six-acre lake landscaped into a natural hollow which reduced the cost as the retaining walls could be constructed more easily.

An act of particular foresight was the decision to have it filled with fresh water rather than planning a marine lake. This has meant that over the years freshwater birds have used the lake, a fact which has taken birdwatchers far too long to appreciate. There are even some who still insist that park lake birdwatching is far too tame for those with a serious interest in the hobby. Here, however, we have seen heron, cormorant, goosander, great crested grebe, goldeneye and a female smew. The birds seem well able to cope with the competition from anglers and with those who just like messing about in boats. The lake is regularly used on winter Sunday mornings by the skillful yachtsmen and women of the BLCC (Blackpool Light Craft Club). Their sails add colour to an already attractive scene.

Stanley Park is far more than just a walk around a lake. There is a county standard cricket ground, many minor pitches as well as football and athletic grounds, tennis courts, bowling and putting greens and magnificent gardens. All these areas can offer real treats for naturalists and here we have seen a common lizard basking in the sun, and on a wet autumn morning a few years ago we watched a black redstart, one of Britain's rarest birds, strutting among the rubble of a wall under repair.

After this sighting many of our friends looked upon Stanley Park in a different light and they now ask a question. Is Stanley Park used to its full potential? We think that the answer is no, especially by those who live on the Fylde. It was built to provide the locals with a winter wonderland, and also as a summer alternative for those wanting to escape the crowds on the Promenade.

Stanley Park should be regarded as a sports complex, a delightful place to walk and shows us clearly that nature and human activities can go on side by side. The planners of the 1920s got it right, and could provide inspiration to some of the modern-day urban architects who far too often seem to be reluctant to learn anything at all from the past.

The Tower Circus is still a feature but now no longer has animal acts, although there is a more traditional circus on the Pleasure Beach. The Tower Circus first brought gasps of excitement on Whit Monday, 1894, and is still content with its world wide reputation for the excellence of its clowns and acrobats.

If the circus is the place for the kids, then which of us of more mature years fails to thrill to the sound of a band in full swing in the ballroom or the sonorous notes of the huge organ which Reginald Dixon made so famous before, during and after the period of

World War II. In addition to the Tower itself the ballroom had yet another French connection and was designed along the same lines as the Paris Opera House. It was opened, in all its magnificence, to an appreciative public in 1899.

The Tower also acted as a natural focus for a host of fringe activities, all of which were amusing even though most were marginally fraudulent and which made up the Golden Mile. Even this now contravenes the Trade Descriptions Act, since the area is certainly less than half a mile but each foot is crammed with showmen intent upon separating the willing holiday makers from their hard earned brass. Here you could, and still can, have your fortune read, but once you could see the bearded lady, watch a honeymoon couple

The Victorian splendour of the Tower Ballroom has been maintained. Reginal Dixon provided daily music for the dancers.

starving to death for love, observe a four-legged, two-headed chicken (which was obviously two badly stuffed birds sewn together), or see the smallest, tallest, thinnest, fattest or most hairy man in the world. The Rector of Stiffkey an "unfrocked Charlaton" could be watched by looking through a hole in the barrel which was said to be his home. Divine retribution came to him at Skegness when, he went, like Daniel, into the Den of Lions. As was the case with young Albert Ramsbottom he "got et". Although the Golden Mile has now lost its gilt edge, some reminder can be enjoyed by visiting Ripley's "Believe it or not Odditorium" near the Pleasure Beach. For those who love Blackpool's history this is a most important haven.

The textile worker could be king for a day by buying champagne on draught from Yates's Wine Lodge near Talbot Square. And what about the waxworks? Louis Tussauds delighted visitors with Shirley Temple, astounded everyone with the muscles of Joe Louis, Blackpool's own pugilist Brian London, who still lives in the town, and later Mohammed Ali. The display brought folk closer to home with Blackpool's own football hero, Stanley Matthews, or frightened those who risked the Chamber of Horrors with the bloody sight of Podmore the mad axe man, or Crippen the first man to be brought to justice as a direct result of a radio message. Toussauds has always managed to keep up to date and among the modern displays are such formidable battlers as Mike Tyson, Frank Bruno and Margaret Thatcher!

Many holiday makers, especially the young, divided their cash into daily doses and once the ration was spent it was off to the beach and to pray for good weather, because lodging houses in the early days insisted that visitors went out after breakfast, returned for their evening meal, and must be in for bed by eleven. There were no bars in the 'digs' and no hanging about the rooms all day getting under the owner's feet.

In good weather the seaside holiday must have been a delight for mill-town kids with smoke in their lungs and with the clatter of looms assaulting their ears. Here they found gentle breezes, the sweet smell of ozone, had the chance to ride on a donkey with its own evocative smell, paddle in the sea and bathe without having to pour water into a tin bath in front of the hearth. They could watch Punch and Judy shows and set about

The Pleasure Beach from the air looked more like a model in the 1960s.

building sand castles and decorating them with flags. What about seashells and ice cream, and the toy windmills which rattled in the slightest of breezes? Tomorrow's money would go on the Pleasure Beach with the terrifying ghost train, throwing darts at cards with a fortune hidden behind them (which no body seemed to hit), or hurling wooden balls at a target. This, when hit dead-centre, operated a trap door which dropped a pretty girl clad in a bathing suit into a pool of water. How daring it was to watch her scramble out!

87

The forty-acre Pleasure Beach is still there and very much up to date with its space invaders and a roller coaster which loops through 360° and does its best to persuade its passengers to become separated from their breakfast!

On the 1st January, 1994, we wrote an article for the Bolton Evening News in which we described our first view of the Pleasure Beach's new attraction, which had already become world famous.

"If you fancy a birdwatching trip early in 1994, you should travel down the M55 motorway and head for Blackpool's south shore. We chose a day of screaming wind following a night of heavy rain but within a couple of minutes we had recorded five cranes, a big dipper and another dipper which is getting bigger by the day. Before you start looking for the ornithological record books we should admit that our first port of call was to Blackpool Pleasure Beach to watch history being made. We had joined hundreds of visitors watching the construction of Blackpool's newest attraction which has not yet been named, but Project 94 is already towering over the Big Dipper which is likely to be relegated to a very little dipper indeed. The latter, however, is still terrifying enough to frighten the life out of us. We shall be content to watch the new ride from a distance. The new Rollercoaster will cost £12 million. The steelwork is being brought from Bolton, assembled at Blackpool Airport and then transported by low loader to the fun park. Eventually it will soar 235 feet (72 metres) above the South Shore and is set to open in the spring of 1995. The project is sponsored by Pepsi-Cola and one of the carriages from the ride is on display outside the pleasure beach, and behind it is a plaque showing what the ride will look like. Each of the carriages will carry thirty brave souls on a mile long journey which will be completed in around two minutes. Your head is likely to arrive thirty seconds in front of your stomach! Whilst we had been watching the cranes at work the sea had been battering away at the promenade, hurling spray high into the air. As the tide ebbed, the beach drained and the vast areas of sand and mud exposed. Onto this feeding area thousands of birds were soon busy building up their food reserves to replace the energy lost during the storm. The gulls including black-headed, herring, lesser black backed, greater black backed and common gulls outnumbered other species, but the variety of these was impressive. We counted more than a thousand dunlin, a delightful little wading bird which feeds by plunging its bill into the mud and sand in search of invertebrates. They feed in flocks and they also fly in formation, twisting and turning as if operted by a single switch. The upper surface of their body is brown whilst the paler belly area catches the sun as they turn during flight and flash like a heliograph. If you are planning an off-peak visit to Blackpool you will be sure of an exciting mixture seeing plenty of wading birds and watching one of the wonders of the fairground world rising above the Pleasure Beach. This is already world famous and a serious rival to Disneyland — in Europe or America — and 1994 looks as if it will surpass all others."

Immediately following its opening, the Pepsi-Max Big One developed operational problems, much of this being associated with ironing out of the complex computer programme. It is now fully functional, a part of the Pleasure Beach's history, the proud heritage of the Thompson family which has always owned this area of beach from its beginning in 1904 and which has given pleasure to millions.

The Pepsi-Max Big One starts to dominate Blakpool's skyline.

The complex was begun by an encampment of gypsies, many of whom were named Boswell and Gypsy Sarah, became famous as a fortune teller. In 1904 the gypsies were removed from their pitch and a pleasure beach was planned which took off like a rocket and has not looked back since.

In addition to new and spectacular attractions, some of the wonderful old rides still exist. Being of a somewhat quiet disposition, we prefer a ride on Sir Hiram Maxim's Captive Flying Machine built in the very early years of the century. This was not just intended as a fairground attraction but was planned to play an important role in the history of aviation. Blackpool was at the forefront of early aviation and, as we have seen, the Warton aerodrome of the British Aircraft Corporation maintains this tradition right up to the present day. Blackpool's Maxim Flying Machine is the only one remaining in use, that at Southport having disappeared long ago.

One famous Blackpool landmark has alas gone, but the Big Wheel built in 1896 still has a magnificent tale to tell, and a remnant of it can still be found in the Fylde. The wheel, situated near the Winter Gardens, was the wonder of the age and had a height of 220 feet (67 metres). The axle which operated the wheel weighed 30 tons. On the opening day in August more than 4,000 people were queueing to take their first ride. Thirty carriages each carrying thirty passengers were rotated from the wheel and provided wonderful views. In 1928 its usefulness was over and it was decided to dismantle the wheel and auction off the carriages. These were put to use as garden sheds and hen cabins but all have been lost save one.

Two nursing sisters named Swallow who ran the Blackpool orphanage bought a carriage and transported it to their cottage near St. Michaels on Wyre. The journey took a pair of heavy horses two days but the structure was soon attached to the cottage and adapted to provide the children from the orphanage an enjoyable holiday. The Big Wheel Cottage can still be seen and was once a popular cafe but is now a private residence, but easily visible from the road and at a suitably discreet distance.

The so-called New Big Wheel was opened in 1990, cost £75,000, is 108 feet (33 metres) high and can rotate 216 passengers within twenty-six carriages in great comfort. This is situated close to the middle of Central Pier and the view from its highest point is spectacular. Close by is the Sandcastle Leisure Centre which opened in 1986 on the site of the former open air baths. In the hot summer of 1995 the centre advertised "cool water" whilst in most English summers they can boast of "warm bathing". In 1996, a full-scale replica of Coronation Street was opened as a Visitors' Centre which is sure of a warm welcome.

A return ride on a tram from the Pleasure Beach all the way to Fleetwood was not to be missed from the day the experimental scheme opened in July, 1898, and attracted over half a million passengers in the first six weeks of the well publicised innovation. Long queues meant quick profits and thus more rolling stock and, despite a few recent threats to cover the tracks and rely on buses, the Blackpool tram is likely to remain for many years despite other resorts having dispensed with theirs. Other towns including Manchester and Sheffield have now turned back the clock and resurrected their tramways. It would seem that Blackpool has been right all along and in 1996 up-dated the system.

One thing which Blackpool has never failed to appreciate is how to successfully blend the old and the new. Nowhere is this better illustrated than the resort's love affair with live theatre. All tastes are catered for with some of the pier shows differing little from the Victorian comics with their "I say, I don't wish to know that . . . kindly leave the stage" patter. There is, however, nothing wrong with this or with the not too skillful magician or ventriloquist. It is here that future stars first learn their craft and then return, perhaps as the top of the bill, to enjoy yet another summer season where they are able try out new routines. There are few better variety shows on offer than those at Blackpool even though the 'Golden Half Mile' has now been 'cleaned up' and replaced by one armed bandits, space invaders and candy floss, Blackpool rock, trinket shops and hot dog stands.

Folk who remember the 1930s and 1940s would, however, still recognize the shellfish stalls and enjoy that unique taste of an oyster slipping down the throat which brought a smile to Dad's lips as he thought of that glass of champagne which he would have at the Wine Lodge when the kids and mum were safely tucked up in bed. One essential visit must still be made to Robert's Oyster Bar on the seafront which has been in continuous operation since it was established in 1876.

At sixty-seven metres, Blackpool's original big wheel was over twice the height of the present wheel, and could accommodate over four times as many passengers.

Many thought they were brave when they bought a hat to keep off the sun which said not 'Kiss Me Quick' but 'Toff for a Week'. The holiday week soon went but there would be next year and — let's just hope the weather would keep fine this time. We remember in the late 1950s travelling to Burnley on a Wakes Special after a blinding hot week and overhearing a badly sunburned lady with a hoard of kids say to her husband with a peeling nose "It can rain nah if it leeks — its Blackburn fair next week!" I expect many an anxious Blackburnian gazed skywards as they emerged from their for once silent mills clutching their holiday pay and praying that Burnley's weather held and that "it hadn't come too soon!".

As bargain foreign holidays, with the certainty of strong sun and cheap drinks and cigarettes, rocketed in popularity, all the British seaside resorts had to withstand an economic depression. Things had to change. Boarding houses became licensed, visitors were given their own keys to come and go as they wished, bathrooms were made 'en suite', foreign dishes appeared on the menu and short stay visitors, even for winter breaks, were welcomed. Cheap (comparatively speaking) travel, shorter working weeks and more generous holidays meant that two holidays and several weekends away to recharge the batteries became popular. There is also an increasing number of modern attractions including the spectacular Sea Life Centre which opened in 1990. Many sealife centres have now been established throughout Britain but Blackpool's, from the viewpoint of visitors numbers, is the most successful. Open throughout the year, the Centre is home to a huge shark but there is also an impressive touch tank and exhibitions showing life in and around the sea at Blackpool.

At Christmas many families find it ideal to move into a Blackpool hotel and enjoy the festivities to the full without having to cook or wash the dishes.

Those who think that Blackpool specialises only in what they loosely describe as "popular entertainment" should take the time to discover what is on offer during the winter. Residents and visitors alike can become 'culture vultures' and enjoy light opera, musical extravaganzas to rival London's West End and the ballet is also a regular attraction.

Visitors even fly into Blackpool these days, Squires Gate being quite adequate for small commercial aircraft. It was from Squires Gate (which is actually in St. Annes) that

Amy Johnson took off on her last flight in an Oxford trainer and came to grief around the Thames Estuary. The resort still derives a substantial part of its revenue from its role as a very successful conference centre, and the presence of the airport helps to ensure this.

Blackpool airport does not compete these days with Gatwick, Heathrow or Manchester but it certainly has a much more impressive history. In June 1909, the French aviator Bleriot flew across the Channel and in October of the same year the first air display in Britain was held at Squires Gate, Blackpool. It is said that 200,000 people attended the four day spectacular. Lord Northcliffe, the owner of the Daily Mail, offered huge prizes and other incentives to pioneer aviators and despite dangerous cross winds the event was a spectacular success. The event got off to a good start with the opening day blessed by warm sunshine and blue sky. British aviation history was certainly begun on the sands of Blackpool and on the site of the present airport.

Blackpool has successfully, and increasingly, extended its season by developing its illuminations, which is a much older concept than is often imagined. Blackpool can truthfully boast that British illuminations were invented by the resort in 1887 when five illuminated tramcars moved up and down the promenade. The idea was actually copied from Berlin's celebrations for the Kaiser's birthday.

Talbot Mews was demolished in the late 1920s to make way for a bus station. Adjacent to the LMS Blackpool North Station, it was frequently packed with new arrivals.

By 1912 'decorative lighting' was a feature of the resort and, although World War I brought the experiment to a halt, there was a spectacular carnival in 1923 after which the idea was resurrected with a vengeance. The lights had to be dimmed when Britain and Germany went to war for a second time in 1939. Blackpool, at that time, became a training camp for British, American and Polish airmen. Many of the latter still live in Blackpool today. The area around Squires Gate became an important assembly point for Wellington Bombers.

In 1949 the lights were back and have become more spectacular each year since. The free show now involves the use of almost 400,000 bulbs of several colours, and lasers strobe into the night sky. Most visitors, however, are willing to contribute to the collecting boxes situated along the promenade.

Trains still come to Blackpool but Central station has been closed and is now a car park. The excursions which fed Central station ran along the line which is now absorbed by the M55 motorway and Yeadon Way which opened in 1986. All that remains of the Railway Age is a wall of the engine sheds and the original toilet block. We now have to rely on the memories of locals who remember the visitors well. Dennis Davidson told us of his "bagging days". As a youngster he earned money with his handcart taking visitors' bags from train to digs. These young entrepreneurs kept diaries in order to keep appointments to collect visitors from their digs and convey their luggage to the station at the end of their holiday.

Coaches and cars are, however, now the main modes of transport and can block the M55 motorway during busy periods. Although some visitors drive straight through and enjoy the free show, many coaches and cars still have to fight for parking space even though the town has been generous with the area allowed for cars. The pubs, including Yates's Wine Lodge, do lucrative, if noisy, business and the Pleasure Beach relies on the lights period to provide around a third of its annual income. Large numbers of visitors choose to take their second holiday at this time and 'No Vacancies' signs adorn the window of almost every guest house, which bring out their Christmas tree bulbs early to add their own contribution to the forest of lights.

We once heard a speaker on holiday resorts refer to Blackpool as brash and vulgar. It transpired that he had been only twice, did not know if the beach was sandy or rocky and thought that all the theatres were populated by 'blue comics' and red faced drunks. He ought to have spent some time in the town and gone to the theatre and thus have this impression quickly dispelled. What a pity he didn't visit on a calm autumn night and walk along the promenade, watch the illuminated piers reflected in the sea and listen to the excited voices of the children as they 'oo and ah' their joy at the flashing tableaux of light telling their favourite fairy stories in a flurry of coloured energy.

Blackpool Central Station in the 1940s. Trippers flooded in from the mill towns — the site is now occupied by car parks.

It does us all good to forget our inhibitions and enjoy ourselves, and Blackpool allows us to do just that. If that is brash and vulgar then so be it!

In 1996 and 1997 serious efforts are being made to bring steam train excursions from the Wakes towns into Blackpool. It may well turn out to be the first new steam railway depot to be constructed for almost eighty years. Could this be yet another 'first' for Blackpool?

CHAPTER SIX:

Thornton, Cleveleys and Fleetwood

In the early 1890s, Blackpool was a thriving resort and Fleetwood, overlooking the important salt exporting estuary of the river Wyre, was also having considerable success. Between the two was once ten miles of wilderness (naturalists would dispute this description) with the last tram stop being at Gynn on Blackpool's northern boundary. Gynn should not be pronounced as in gin but as in ginnel. It meant a narrow pathway leading through the areas having the Fylde's only cliffs to the sea. From the Gynn Hotel there is a splendid stroll down to the promenade and the views across the cliffs can be spectacular in a high tide. Birdwatchers and anglers are all happy battling with the elements.

Both Blackpool and Fleetwood wanted to be linked by tram and, as always, necessity proved to be the mother of invention, although on this occasion two fairy godpersons were needed in the forms of Benjamin Sykes and Thomas Lumb. Their scheme (or perhaps drive for profits) was enhanced by their contacts with local families who owned land between Blackpool and Fleetwood. Rossall and Thornton estates co-operated to ensure that the land on which Cleveleys now stands could be linked by electric tram. Sykes himself owned a stretch of land called Eryngo Lodge which he wished to develop as a hydropathic complex. Eryngo was the old English name for sea holly. This plant had

Opposite: *Fleetwood as it appeared in 1838, featuring the impressive architecture of Decimus Burton.*

97

Thomas Hawthornwaite (in the straw hat), Thornton's last working miller, can be seen entering his mill c.1920.

substantial roots which could be boiled in honey and used as a sweet in Tudor times before chocolate was discovered.

Closer to Blackpool, the Norbreck estates controlled the land around Bispham through which the tramway would have to pass. Guess who had control over Norbreck? Benjamin Sykes! This left only the stretch of flower be-decked dunes between Gynn and Bispham to be won over, but this time the advisor to the estate was not Sykes. It was, however, Thomas Lumb. Thus the route was easily planned and trams soon began to rattle through the dunes on their way to Fleetwood, and have done so ever since.

The area around Cleveleys was now ripe for development and by 1906 a model village was planned and this is still the impression given, just as it is at Lever's Port Sunlight on the banks of the Mersey. The Fylde development requires a little more imagination, however, but its unique design is there for those with eyes to see. Cleveleys has a flat sandy beach from which swimming is popular and safety is ensured by an efficient "Bay Watch type" lifeguard system. Picnic sites are a feature and provide a quiet alternative from Blackpool's more crowded shoreline. Angling is also a popular activity on the beach at Cleveleys, especially during the colder months. There is a boating lake, miniature railway and several amusement arcades but which are cleverly hidden away. Cleveleys' advantage is that there are still enough quiet places into which it is possible to escape and find peace in the company of soaring skylarks and dune flowers including heartsease pansy, lady's bedstraw and the delicate blue nodding blooms of harebells.

Inland from the new settlement is the much older village of Thornton, watched over by Marsh Windmill — its red sails contrasting with the white painted brickwork and surrounded by colourful flower beds. The 70-foot (21·3-metre) structure was built in 1794 and, although it has not worked since 1922, it is still open to the public. The last working miller was Thomas Hawthornthwaite; one of our uncles gave us a photograph of Thomas wearing a straw hat and entering his mill.

Whenever we have been battered, buffeted and bemused by wind we always make a point of visiting the coast in the lull which follows the storm. Birds out at sea have no protection from the wind and are driven ashore, exhausted by their battering. This ensures excellent watching.

There was still a strong wind as we focused our binoculars on the shore below Rossall Point near Fleetwood. Birds were everywhere, feathers still ruffled by the wind but intent upon feeding in order to replace the energy lost during their unequal battle with the elements. There were dunlin, oyster catcher, knot, redshank, shelduck and thousands of very bad tempered gulls. These habitats all need conserving.

Conservation does not just relate to natural history — buildings are also important and none more so than when it involves Britain's fast diminishing number of windmills.

From the windy shore we made our way to Marsh Mill for two reasons. Firstly, we wanted to see how the grand old mill had stood up to two days of fierce winds, but also because it is now the focus for a complex of craft shops, cosy little coffee shops and a pub, which is just the place to recover from a session on the shore.

Windmills must have at least four floors, but the majority, including Thornton, have six. The top floor is roofed by a revolving cap which carries the main sails and also a smaller set of sails called the Fantail which operate to turn the main sails into the wind. Keeping the sails turning was one of the miller's main problems, but he also had to stop them turning too quickly. From our position near the cap we were shown the huge breaking system by our knowledgeable guide. Machinery made of wood and revolving too quickly soon builds up frictional heat and is a fire risk.

The sacks of grain were hauled up to the fifth floor of the windmill on hoists. So that the strain of the pulling does minimum damage to the structure of the mill tower the winch is secured to the wall by an iron hook which penetrates through to the outside. If you look at a windmill you will often see a metal "S" shape embedded in the outside wall. The weight pulling against this metal keeps pulling the walls in the correct position.

The grain is fed into a hopper leading down to the millstones which do the grinding. This process is the same in both windmills and watermills. The grain is ground between the 'runner stone' which is rotated by the wind-driven machinery and has a hole through its centre for the grain to pass. The 'bedstone' remains still as the grinding proceeds. The setting of the gap between the stones has always been a skilled job.

The grain then feeds down into sacks. The use of stones for grinding produces very rough brown "stone ground" flour. These were eventually replaced by steam driven steel rollers and these produce very much finer white flour. When white flour was first produced it was said to be more healthy than the "crude flour". We have now come full circle and many people insist on brown bread which, as the TV advert insists, "Has nowt teken out".

Just after the First World War it seemed inevitable that Blackpool would eventually absorb Cleveleys, but, in the event, this was not the way things developed. Thornton and Cleveleys joined the Borough of Wyre and, along with its main resort at Fleetwood, developed a holiday character quite distinct from that of Blackpool.

Fleetwood became three towns in one — a fishing centre, a thriving port and, importantly in the context of this book, a much under-rated holiday resort. It has been suggested that Fleetwood ought to make up its mind, but it is quite entitled to enquire why it should. The interplay between the three fascinating aspects provides a unique appeal for those who want a seaside holiday with a difference.

Modern Fleetwood began as one man's dream. The Hesketh-Fleetwood family had resided at Rossall Point for centuries, their hall now forming an integral part of Rossall School. The family were staunchly Catholic during Tudor and Stuart times and suffered a great deal of persecution because of their beliefs. There were, however, survivors and in the 1830s Sir Peter Hesketh-Fleetwood could still look out over a vast estate partly composed of an expanse of sand and salt marsh surrounding the estuary of the river Wyre, with its vast underground deposits of salt. These have since been tapped by ICI which has a large complex at Thornton, and they provided an incentive to keep the channel dredged. The Wyre is, therefore, still navigable and is not silting up like the Ribble, Dee or the Lune. Listening to the music of the marsh birds, Sir Peter had a dream which, as things turned out, was eventually to bankrupt him; but the very real presence of his town would seem to vindicate the sense of his initial reasoning.

By 1836 the railroad from Preston had been planned to reach the desolate marsh at the river mouth, and the cul-de-sac to be so created was ready to receive its new town. Sir Peter employed one of the best known architects of the period to design his town — Decimus Burton who had been a pupil of the great John Nash. Burton already had an impressive record in the design of seaside towns, and buildings at St. Leonards and Hove had their origins on his drawing board. London's Regents Street is also a Burton masterpiece.

Burton can never have been given a better brief than that of a free hand to design a complete town from scratch, but there was the problem of time, for Sir Peter was in a hurry. Decimus was reputed to have reacted by hiring a horse-drawn plough and using this to mark out the streets. He based his plan around a sand dune which he renamed the Mount and from which the new streets radiated. The area was once known as Tup Hill and was obviously previously used as an area where sheep were grazed and the ewes and tups were mated.

Although speed was of the essence, this was no jerry building job and some fine buildings, including St. Peters Church, Queens Terrace and the North Euston Hotel, complete with soaring Doric columns, remain to prove it. Any town with the intention of becoming a port needs a lighthouse and Burton designed two delightfully unusual structures. He seems to have enjoyed himself with the smaller building, which looks like a pepper pot, surrounded by a balustrade and this has always had the dual function of a promenade shelter and a light. The second, much larger and probably more efficient, is the Pharos, strategically, but also artistically, placed at the junction of Lune and Pharos Streets.

Actually, four lighthouses feature in the history of this coastline. A structure known as the Rossall Landmark was mentioned in the Domesday Book. There were many subsequent structures and a substantial rebuild was required in 1848, with another needed ten years later following storm damage. The light was kept in repair by the Lancaster Port Authority. It was finally demolished in 1924 but the other three structures have been of more recent importance.

Lighthouse-keeper Jack Cross prepares to spend his eleventh successive Christmas at the Fleetwood Lighthouse in 1938.

During the construction of his new port Sir Peter Fleetwood-Hesketh knew that good navigation was essential and he commissioned an expert on this subject to advise him. Captain Henry Mangles Denham RN suggested two inland and one seaward lights. These had to be lined up by approaching ships which were thus kept away from the dangerous shallows.

In 1840, the same year that the railway opened, the three lights were simultaneously switched on, and the locals cheered as they saw the new lights beaming out into the darkening sky.

The Wyre light has been a nostalgic spot ever since its construction, and it remained in operation until 1948 when fire damaged it and the keepers were taken off the sandbank. A remote-controlled light was placed nearby. The Railway Company operated the light and, long after his retirement, we talked to Jack Cross who always seemed to be on duty during the 1930s even over the Christmas period. There is an historic photograph taken in 1938 showing Jack's supplies being delivered at low water. The remnant of the old light still remains, looking skeleton-like on the isolated sand banks.

Decimus Burton's two inland lights have been treated much more kindly by Father Time. The large light is 90 feet (27·5 metres) high and the beam is visible thirteen miles out to sea. The original cost was £1,480. The smaller lighthouse situated closer to the shore was almost as expensive and cost £1,375. Both the structures were built by John Tomkinson but obviously to the design of Decimus Burton.

In the early days, Fleetwood had no accommodation for the workers and they were obliged to travel daily, many coming from Preston by stagecoach. By 1844 the railway had arrived and steamers were leaving Fleetwood for the Isle of Man, Whitehaven and also to Ardrossan, giving a comparatively rapid and lucrative route into Scotland. Queen Victoria returned to the affairs of state in London, following a holiday in Scotland, via Fleetwood. The North Euston Hotel is still the most impressive hostelry in Fleetwood. The year 1847, which looked like a milestone in Sir Peter's business affairs, turned into a millstone around his neck; for this was the year that the rail link over Shap was opened and the town almost immediately lost all of its influence over the Scottish trade.

Sir Peter's resources were not unlimited and he had to sell land to continue to develop his town, but even this cash ran out with his magnificent dream only half finished. He even had to sell the North Euston, which for a time was an army barracks. When the sad and unlucky man died in 1866, the Fleetwood Estate Company took over and shifted the emphasis towards trade and the high building standards were relaxed. This is why Burton's buildings are now surrounded by others designed to be merely functional with the artistic aspects far too expensive to be contemplated. This philosophy is easily understood, as survival was the name of the game during that period of the town's history.

In 1878 the railway companies financed the construction of an extensive dock complex and in the 1890s Grimsby trawler owners established a deep-water fishery which obtained most of its catch from the waters around Iceland and needed a west coast base.

Fleetwood had been an important fishing port from around 1860 and by the 1870s almost one hundred vessels berthed there were earning a good living. 'Serious' deep-water and long-distance fishing began in 1889 when a vessel, appropriately called 'The Stormcock', brought a load of mackerel and kippered herring into Fleetwood, which at that time was mainly concerned with other imports, especially grain and timber. At about the same time 'Lark', the first steam trawler, chugged into the dock. Soon the timber pond and the grain elevator had to be sacrificed in order to serve the demands for more and more fish.

Fleetwood around 1895. Photograph taken from the top of the grain elevator.

Fleetwood had an advantage over many other ports as it was closer to the fishing grounds and already had a railway network. The industrial areas, including the Wakes towns, had an insatiable demand for fish to go with their chips.

We have a number of good friends who were once trawler skippers and who have become what academics would call "Piscatorial Historians". They would describe themselves as being "in love with a dying industry". The big trawlers were no threat to the local fishermen as there were three distinct types of fishing operation out of Fleetwood as at other major ports such as Aberdeen, Hull and Grimsby which were all on the east coast.

At Fleetwood there were inshore fishing boats, mostly family owned, and crewed by two or three which landed prawns and flat fish. The Middle Water Trawlers worked out of Morecambe Bay but were quite prepared to head out to Scottish Waters, even to the Faroes and perhaps as far as Iceland, but this was the exception rather than the rule. Catches here included hake, whiting, cod and even ray, which is a member of the shark family. These trawlers, however, specialised in hake and this is still the case, although recent restrictions in catches have caused problems and hardship to the men and their families.

The Distant Water Trawlers had crews of about twenty real tough guys who could remain at sea in Arctic weather conditions for up to a month. They fished around Iceland, the White Sea, Bear Island and off the coast of Norway. Catches included plaice, sole, cod, haddock and our particular favourite halibut, which tastes like fish but bites like steak!

Fleetwood was badly affected by the closure of its rail-link in 1970, but particularly following the so called Cod War and EEC regulations which did British fishermen no favours at all. Fleetwood fared so badly that it seems that the only Fisherman's Friends to have survived the heady days of the trawling fleet are those working at Lofthouses factory which still produces the lozenges which are world famous. The aroma of these tablets permeates the atmosphere around the docks, part of which is now developing as a marina for pleasure craft.

The grain elevator soon after construction in 1893. It contained 143 storage silos, each of 200 tons capacity. The "ship's leg", for extracting grain from ships's holds, can be seen on the left.

Fisherman's Friends roll off the production line.

In 1865 James Lofthouse, a Fleetwood Pharmacist, was so popular with fishermen seeking relief from bronchial complaints that his shop became too small. Initially, James produced a liquid but this presented a problem as the glass bottles were too often broken during rough seas. James Lofthouse rose to the occasion by soaking the liquid in a rich dough and then pressing them into a liquid made up of liquorice, capsicum, eucalyptus and menthol. The precise formula remains a secret and the Lofthouse family still direct operations from Fleetwood. The 'Friends', at first restricted to the Fleetwood Trawlermen, have now been marketed throughout the world and Doreen Lofthouse and her sons, Tony and Duncan, are following the strong family tradition.

Sucking a Fisherman's Friend must have reminded the seamen of a warm and welcoming home port, but alas some did not survive these dangerous voyages. Just opposite the North Euston Hotel, and on the promenade close to the Low Lighthouse is a memorial to those lost at sea.

The Fisherman's Friend tram ready for the Blackpool Illuminations

Fleetwood fish is still guaranteed to bring a glint to the eye of Lancashire's fish and chip connoisseurs, and many a day tripper returned home with a bundle of fish and lots of other goodies from the market which well deserves its bustling reputation.

The Icelandic 'fish war' and the new trend towards frozen fish obviously hit Fleetwood hard, but a taste of the good times can be savoured by a visit to the town museum situated on Dock Street. This listed building was constructed by Benjamin Whitworth in 1863 and bought and presented to the town as a free library by Samuel Fielden in 1887. There are exhibitions of both deep sea and inshore fishing, as well as traditional methods of cockling, musselling, shrimping and salmon netting. We have had many an interesting conversation with Simon Heyhoe the curator of Natural History who is becoming increasingly optimistic about the town and the wildlife which surrounds it.

The crews of trawlers from Fleetwood, Hull and Grimsby faced great dangers during icy voyages. Here the vessel 'Notts County' has been abandoned on the coast of Iceland. Insurance assessors are braving the weather in the early 1970s.

Also in the museum we had many interesting conversations with Ian Baxter who is the official historian, and one-time employee, of the ICI chemical plant at Thornton. Ian has helped the museum to set up a very impressive display concerned with the history of salt which includes a very realistic salt mine.

Whilst the salt mines of Siberia are still infamous, those of the Wyre are now confined to history. This salt-based industry, however, still provides the Fylde with a large slice of its income. It is hard to imagine that the giant ICI complex at Thornton had such simple beginnings, and even these were based on the opposite side of the Wyre around Preesall.

Salt is still important to the area. A railway wagon containing Fleetwood salt — by this time the salt works were taken over by ICI

Salt has been a vital commodity since before written history, and salt roads led from the known deposits all over Britain. Part of a Roman soldier's pay was in salt. The Latin for salt is Salarium from which our word salary has evolved.

Until the mid-nineteenth century salt was used to preserve meat, but during the Industrial Revolution a huge business developed producing large numbers of now essential products from salt. ICI at Thornton still provides around 1,500 salaries to the people of the Fylde, and the knock-on effect to the service industries is immense.

To discover the history of salt extraction, Ian guided us to the area around Preesall. He told us that salt was laid down more than 200 million years ago as shallow seas evaporated in the hot climate. In 1872 a Barrow-in-Furness based haematite company searching for iron ore at Preesall discovered rich deposits of salt. These drillings were carried out by an American of Swedish extraction named Charles Olsen who had learned his craft drilling for oil. Ian showed us his grave in Preesall cemetery.

A drilling rig of a salt mine at Pressell near Fleetwood.

The site of the first shaft is now almost smothered beneath a tangle of elder, alder, bramble and dog rose, but we were able to clear a space around this historic site.

By 1893 rock salt was being conveyed to Preesall jetty via a railway, the old track of which we were able to follow. Eventually, this was linked to the Knott End railway but essential rail communications were still better on the Fleetwood side of the river.

By the 1890s brine was also being produced and piped across the river Wyre to the Fleetwood Salt Works. The coal needed to produce the heat to evaporate the brine to crystalline salt was more easily brought by rail to the Fleetwood side of the river.

The demand for salt quickly increased and the Preesall Rock Salt Mine worked until 1930, whilst the extraction of brine only ceased during 1994. Raw materials are now brought in from Cheshire via the road network.

The Fleetwood Salt Company joined the Salt Union in 1888. In 1890 the salt works was taken over by the United Alkali Company. By 1926 ICI was in control of the complex.

In 1930 the Preesall Rock Salt Mine was proving ever more difficult to operate with flooding the major problem, but subsidence was also an embarrassment. Ian showed us flooded areas called the Flash and the well-named Big Hole. This is now a wildfowl haven and lies at the junction between the salt railway and the route to the Pilling and Knott End Railway.

Here we watched greylag geese, moorhen, Canada geese, mallard, coot and swans. Nearby we grubbed about in the nettles and the brambles before discovering the ruins of the old salt mine and the loading shoots associated with it. We also found the capped head of a brine well now rusting away but with the wheel controlling the mechanism still clearly visible.

Although the Preesall brine wells have now been shut down for ever, a supply of fresh water for the Thornton complex is still being pumped across the Wyre. In front of the offices and pumping station is the reservoir, surrounded by reeds and the haunt of a couple of elegant mute swans.

We re-crossed the river via the Knott End Ferry and returned to the museum which is only a short distance from the terminus of the tramway. Fleetwood trams, unlike Blackpool's, share the road with normal traffic and do not have a thoroughfare to themselves. We have seen many tourists driving with panic in their eyes when a tram heads straight towards them. These giants are assured of the right of way for more reasons than one!

Despite trade taking a great deal of Fleetwood's energy, the holiday resort aspect to its character is always apparent. The long promenade runs southwards to Cleveleys and the usual facilities such as the boating lake, the largest model-yacht pool in Europe, swimming pool and colourful gardens are as attractive as those of other resorts. The beach in this area is flat and safe, whilst life guards ensure that the adventurous keep clear of the northern end where currents around the Wyre estuary are treacherous. Fleetwood pier, built in 1910, is short but in much better condition than those of many other seaside towns. This is probably due to the fact that the seaward end is used as a landing jetty whilst nearer to the land the amusement arcade provides what has become traditional pier entertainment.

Few resorts have anything to match Fleetwood's Marine Hall complex surrounded by lovely gardens, set around an outdoor bar. There is a 700-seater hall which can be used either for conferences or entertainment. A new leisure centre on the seafront has an excellent swimming pool and a spacious sports hall. There are two golf courses, one at Fleetwood itself, the other across the river Wyre at Knott End.

We love walks which are full of history, industrial archeology and natural history. When the walk is described in a colourful and free leaflet designed by the local authority then we are in Heaven.

We have spent many a happy walk around the Wyreside Ecology Centre in the company of Len Blacow the warden. From the Centre a delightful footpath runs to Skippool whilst on the opposite bank Wardley Creek can be clearly seen. Before Fleetwood was constructed Wardley and Skippool were busy ports controlled from the Customs House at Poulton-Le-Fylde. When this complex was in full swing all that could be seen in the Fleetwood area was a deep pool known as Canstie Hole which Sir Peter Fleetwood later developed into his main dockland area.

In the period around 1750, the Poulton Customs House handled more cargo than Liverpool and imports included rum, tobacco, sugar, wine, cotton, oranges and especially timber from such far off places as North America, West Indies, the Baltic and Imperial Russia. South West Africa was also an important customer as bird excrement, known as guano, was brought to enrich the land which was being reclaimed from the drained fenlands of the Fylde.

There is a goodly quantity of local guano still produced in the area by the thousands of birds which are found in and around the Wyre estuary, whatever the state of the tide or the time of the year.

One of our favourite birdwatching trips is to cross the mouth of the estuary from Fleetwood via the Knott End Ferry, which itself has a fascinating history. There is no doubt that local fishermen were always prepared to row passengers across the Wyre in order to earn a few pennies. Travellers were equally willing to pay in order to avoid the sixteen-mile round trip via Shard Bridge. Shard is a Scandinavian word meaning 'shallows'. The ferry, however, was always dependent upon whether there was anyone free at the time to undertake the trip. There was always a strident demand for a regularly timetabled ferry service, and the Fleetwood Express dated 5th July, 1893, complained that:

> "There is no regular ferry service . . . and
> no means of ferry transport for cattle,
> horses and vehicles . . . [and] . . .
> Fleetwood . . . is practically cut off from the
> other side of the Wyre."

Eventually the ferry service became a vital link and on 14th August, 1905, 10,200 people crossed the Wyre. These days, the ferry only operates during the summer months but this should be celebrated because there have been several occasions when the service almost ceased altogether.

During the 1950s the steam ferry *Wyresdale* was a marvellous vessel and we remember many a yarn with the skipper, and were very upset when we heard the news on 12th April 1957, that her boiler had exploded. She was considered to be uneconomic to repair and was sold.

In the 1990s we tried several times to find a picture of her and following an appeal in our newspaper column of the Evening Gazette, Harry Hill sent photographs taken in 1952. She was indeed a wonderful vessel and the last one capable of carrying large numbers of passengers;

The Knott Ferry heading out from Fleetwood. This photograph, kindly given to me by Mr Harry Hill, was probably taken in 1952.

she was commissioned in 1925. Her peak year was 1947 when she carried 1,432,856 people. There is still something romantic and mysterious about crossing water and many ramblers find that a ferry trip adds extra enjoyment to their walks.

The Wyre Borough Council has produced an excellent Circular Walk on the opposite side of the river around Knott End which is nearly four miles (6 kms) in total. On a cold winter's morning we began our stroll alongside the Wyre estuary and the tide was just coming in as we focused our binoculars on the shore.

Wading birds seemed to be everywhere with oyster catchers being particularly dominant but there were plenty of ringed plover, dunlin, knot, turnstone and a goodly number of curlew.

After passing the golf links, where many sportsmen were playing and ignoring the icy cold wind, we reached Hackensall which is surely the most under-rated hall in the whole of Lancashire. The house is privately owned and so walkers should always ensure that they respect the privacy of the people who live there. There are, however, splendid views of the hall from the footpath.

There has been an occupied site around the hall from at least Roman times and in Victorian times a huge hoard of Roman coins was found. It is said that there was once an important Roman port at Knott End; this was marked on a famous map drawn by the historian Ptolemy. The refuge was known as Portus Setantiorum.

The Vikings also made good use of the Wyre estuary and it is said by many historians that the name Hackensall comes from the Scandinavian name of Hakon. By the eleventh century, the Anglo-Saxon lords of Preesall built a fortified dwelling to keep out invading Vikings but the present hall dates to the seventeenth century. There is evidence, however, of some earlier dwellings perhaps even dating back to Norman times, d a very ancient chapel was found in the grounds.

From Hackensall, a signpost indicates the way to Barnaby Sands and Burrows Marsh both of which are attractive and important to the fauna and flora. This is shown by the fact that the area has been designated an SSSI (Site of Special Scientific Interest). Here we saw a weasel on the hunt, and the birds were particularly wary. Our list included redshank, shelduck, greenfinch and lapwings by the hundred. Birds of prey were also present and we watched a hunting short-eared owl almost hovering over the marshes.

We did expect to find lots of birds but we did not, at this time, expect to find the Pilling Pig. Actually, this was not an animal but a railway. The Pig was named because the locals compared the first railway engines with the sound of a screaming pig. The railway opened in 1870 to provide a link between Garstang and Knott End. It was never very profitable and eventually fell victim to the Beeching cuts of the 1960s.

Part of the old line now follows the footpath and leads back alongside the Knott End Golf Club. This is a wonderful winter walk. On Sundays there is often a market at Knott End and there are also a number of hotels and cafes.

From Knott End we looked out over the estuary towards Fleetwood on the opposite bank and as the tide came in large numbers of yachts with colourful sails could be seen, their crews enjoying the crisp breeze. They are always a hardy lot these sailors and so are the birds which were massing on the mud flats.

Another footpath follows the river Wyre inland for a distance of almost four miles to Hambleton, whilst another follows the shell strewn shoreline to Pilling Marshes. Here, winter bird-watchers gather to watch flocks of wild geese which feed upon the lush grasses. Beyond Pilling is yet another historic estuary. The Lune flows through Lancaster and is guarded on the south by Glasson and to the north by Sunderland Point. Beyond Sunderland lies Morecambe and Heysham, the last of Old Lancashire's western seaside resorts.

In the early 1960s, Fleetwood was on the verge of losing its Isle of Man ferry. This was but one of the problems faced by the town.

The port of Heysham finally won the battle with Fleetwood to secure the passenger ferry service to Ireland and the Isle of Man. We have a photograph taken in the early 1960s when the passenger service was in decline, but the port has continued to run a valuable freight service across the Irish Sea, and the 'roll on roll off' ferries are very much still a feature of this fascinating town. Its architecture, its history and its atmosphere are all unique and Fleetwood should never be under-estimated.

CHAPTER SEVEN:

Morecambe

O n the sandy coast where the resort of Morecambe now stands, four tiny villages once earned their living from fishing and especially from shrimping and musselling. It would seem that the coastline was much more rocky in the past and commercial mussel beds were a feature of the bay. Sand and silt, however, have since covered some of the skeers and this, combined with increased pollution, once reduced the mussel fishing almost to extinction, although shrimps were, and are still, taken commercially all over the vast expanse of the Bay. In recent years, however, pollution levels have fallen and mussel fishing is now returning commercially. Codling and whitebait are also local delicacies.

When the first Ordnance Survey map was drawn up in 1848, the villages of Poulton-le-Sands, Torrisholme, Bare and Heysham were all marked, whilst the name Morecambe was restricted to the Bay itself and was not associated with any specific settlement. Poulton Ring Point was marked and it was here that around 1850 the old stone jetty was built, whilst also indicated was Shore Cottage on the site now occupied by the Clock Tower.

It is still possible to see some remnant of Poulton-le-Sands as a village right in the heart of Morecambe and just inland from the Gala Bingo Hall. The market, which is to be re-located during the late 1990s, occupied the site of Poulton Hall which was sadly demolished in 1932. During the fifteenth and sixteenth centuries the hall was one of the

Opposite: *Morecambe Promenade in the early 1950s.*

homes of the Washington family and the area thus has great significance for Americans. This should be an incentive for tourists from the States, especially as Morecambe is so close to the Lake District and the historic city of Lancaster. Many such visitors will no doubt remark that the other north-western resorts may be less impressive than the theme parks of the States, but Morecambe's cultural links are well forged. One impressive remnant of Poulton Hall remains in the form of the old ornate doorway near which is a plaque, almost hidden by ivy and other greenery, and which is situated close to the rear of Morecambe Town Hall where parking is free.

Look out also for the nearby Poulton Square, which is a clear reminder of the old village, containing fishermen's cottages and a solid looking farmhouse bearing a datestone of 1687. A corner shop still sells fish and thus provides the last remaining link with the original working village of Poulton-le-Sands.

Heysham, however, is the best known of the villages from an historical point of view and it is still a quaint mixture of geography, history, custom and folklore. The narrow village street winds its colourful and cheerful way down to the rocky foreshore with its rich coating of seaweeds and fascinating rock pools, all very reminiscent of Cornish fishing hamlets. The shops which line the streets sell the usual seaside trinkets but the unique feature is the famous nettle beer. Since the Trades Descriptions Act the brew cannot officially be called 'beer' and it now has to be called 'nettle drink'. What we want to know is how they get away with the name ginger 'beer' which has a similar taste to the nettle drink!

Visitors of a genteel disposition have long loved Heysham, although much adverse publicity has been generated by the opening of the nuclear power stations. A visitors' centre which opened in 1995 will do much to improve the image of the power station but those firmly opposed to nuclear energy will never be convinced of its safety. The four reactors at Heysham generate the power to satisfy the whole of Lancashire and a substantial proportion of that demanded by Greater Manchester. The new centre opens daily from April to October from 10 am to 5 pm and for the rest of the year from 11 am to 4 pm. There are guided tours, with the last circuit taking place 1½ hours before closing. There is so much to see, and there are also computer graphics, displays and videos as well as a tour of the reactor gallery and the control room. Entry to the centre is free of charge and there is also a nature centre which we had the pleasure of opening in 1993. There have been regular censuses of birds around the area, and numbers have been steadily increasing since the station was opened. Those who are opposed to nuclear power do need to examine these statistics with an open mind and with an eye for scientific accuracy rather than sensationalism!

Morecambe in full swing in the early 1960s.

Heysham village is still a 'civilised' place with lots of tea shops and usually quiet pubs and with the headland overlooked by Morecambe, its bay and the majestic Lakeland mountains. Morecambe itself does not have an historic church, but this is more than compensated for by the two ancient gems at Heysham. St. Peters, set on the site of an eighth-century church, is now mainly of fourteenth century construction but it was restored in the seventeenth. From it, it is possible to see the ship building town of Barrow-in-Furness, where one of us was born, and beyond it on a fine day the gentle contours of the Isle of Man. The churchyard and its surrounds are always attractive, especially so in the spring when there are spectacular displays of yellow and purple crocuses.

Beyond St. Peters, along a path strewn during the warmer months with wild flowers, are the ruins of what is often stated to be Lancashire's first church. It is dedicated to St. Patrick and is perched on a rocky outcrop. It is less than 30 feet long and 10 feet (9 metres by 3 metres) wide and was founded by the Irish Christians during the sixth, seventh and eighth centuries. The soil was so thin that the graves around it could not be dug deep and body shaped holes had to be hewn into the solid rock. Eight such graves can clearly be seen, including one hacked out for a child. The Celtic church may have suffered during the Viking raids but, in time, even the hard living, heavy drinking and rapacious sea dogs saw the light and were converted to the Christian faith.

Within St. Peters church is a typical 'hogs back shaped' gravestone which dates to the tenth century. This has Christian symbols on one side and pagan insignia on the other, which shows that the Vikings were not absolutely certain of their conversion and preferred to hedge their bets!

The proposal to build a Heritage Centre in Heysham village is both imaginative and sensible. There is plenty of land available around Heysham Head, which was once a popular tourist attraction, and both the ancient and modern history, as well as the splendid views over the bay, will add one more amenity to Morecambe.

Once the villages were combined into a marketable seaside resort, it was soon realised that profits were essential for growth and communications had to be the best and most reliable that expertise and money could provide.

The area around Poulton-le-Sands became a popular bathing spot and a thriving port also evolved. Steamboats were moored at the "old" pier which was built during the 1830s. This was, however, often useless as silting up increased and the water became gradually more shallow. Services ran to Londonderry, Belfast and Dublin but they were anything but reliable, and there was a sarcastic local saying that anyone who turned up late was operating on "steam boat time".

When the Central pier was built there was some increase in the depth of water, but sand was still encroaching and there was an obvious need for a reliable deep water harbour. The solution was eventually found at Heysham, and for several years before the harbour opened in 1904 the tranquility of the village was disrupted as hard working, and even harder drinking, labourers constructed the vital docks in double-quick time. The new complex got the vote over Fleetwood as the linking port for Belfast and this directly assisted the development of Morecambe as a holiday resort, and many an Irish family enjoyed a summer break on the coast of England.

With the re-development of Morecambe in the late 1990s it is quite possible that this could happen all over again. Day trips to the Isle of Man also gave Morecambe holidaymakers a feeling of having been on a cruise. Our family have always been avid writers of postcards and we found an impressive collection written in 1905 during their first "holiday passage" to Douglas, when the Isle of Man was a global experience! The horse drawn trams which still operate along the promenade at Douglas were once also a feature of Morecambe. A return to this form of transport would, we think, be an asset to Morecambe. There is, however, a major problem. The infrastructure of a modern town involves water piping, electricity and telephone cabling and the construction of tram lines would involve massive expenditure.

The Port of Heysham is still busy with freight particularly dealing with Ireland, and there is also now a substantial trade in oil and natural gas. This, and the power station, have reduced the popularity of Heysham Head and Half Moon Bay but there are signs that both areas, which were once honeypots for Morecambe's visitors, are recovering and tourist numbers are gradually building up once more.

Beyond Heysham is Middleton Sands which is within walking distance of one of the most historic and fascinating ports to be found anywhere in Britain — Sunderland Point. Winter or summer, spring or fall, morning, noon or night, the walk across to Sunderland is magical. In winter, short-eared owls and peregrines dive among the host of waders and wildfowl, and provide naturalists with an unforgettable experience. In summer, larks soar high in joyful song over the salt marsh, coloured by the pink carpets of thrift and white masses of scurvy grass which was once collected by sailors and which was chewed during their long voyages. The plant is rich in vitamin C and was the only defence against the dreaded disease of scurvy. Scurvy grass only went out of fashion when the British Navy began to carry fresh limes, which are even richer in vitamin C. Limes were first used during the period of the American Wars of Independence and this is why the 'Yanks' still refer to the British as "Limeys".

Buried close to the shore is "Sambo", a negro whose marked but unconsecrated grave is still supplied with gifts of wild flowers by local well-wishers. We would suggest that he has a happier resting place than those of more wealth and influence who are interred amid a cluster of thousands of ugly tombstones. Give us a sea breeze and bird song anytime!

Beyond Sambo's resting place lies the old port of Sunderland, which was planned by a Quaker named Robert Lawson who realised that substantial profits could be made by trading in North America, and especially in the West Indies. Cotton, tobacco and slaves were the main source of income. Towards the end of the seventeenth century the quay was beginning to take shape; a warehouse (now converted into attractive flats) still stands and bears the date 1707. By 1728 Lawson had taken one risk too many and became bankrupt; his once proud port gradually silted up, slowly languished and is now a wonderful museum piece. At one time the complex of ports around Lancaster was second in importance, with only Bristol in front of it.

Sunderland Point did flirt with the possibility of becoming a bathing resort. In 1804 a Mrs. Coupland was advertising a cottage to let via the columns of the *Lancaster Gazette* and Sunderland also had two hostelries which also catered for folk of "quality". Both of these are now private residences because the "bathers of quality" found nearby Morecambe (then still called Poulton-le-Sands) to have a much greater area of clean sand, a gently sloping beach and easier communications.

Initially, Morecambe was designed as a port to compensate for the inevitable loss of Lancaster and perhaps also Sunderland Point and Glasson Dock as the Lune estuary silted up. The Morecambe Harbour and Railway Act which was passed in 1846 involved the construction of a rail link just to the south of Poulton-le-Sands. By 1848 the line was extended to the old stone pier, and also to a now vanished wooden jetty, and goods were transferred to and from ships bound for Scotland, Ireland and even as far afield as the Baltic and Spain. Eventually the unreliable tides, plus the building of the Furness railway to link a deep water harbour between Piel Island and Roa Island off Barrow-in-Furness, robbed Morecambe of its commerce. What Lancashire stole from Morecambe, however, the Yorkshire towns restored in ample measure.

The Railway Age persuaded the hard working classes to travel just for leisure and a direct link was forged between the Yorkshire woollen towns such as Halifax and Leeds, but especially with Bradford. A scenic route brought trippers via Skipton and Hellifield, which was the major junction, and thence via Settle, Bentham and Carnforth to the breezy, healthy open spaces of Morecambe Bay.

The developing resort, especially the area around the Battery, became so popular with the Tyke mill workers that for many years Morecambe was called "Bradford By the Sea" and also "Little Bradford". Battery Point was, as its name implies, an old cannon emplacement and around it was a shingle bank fringed with salt marshes and the haunt of huge numbers of wading birds and wildfowl. Great congregations of birds gathered from Battery Point

The refurbished Old Stone Jetty.

and along the long stretch leading north towards Hest Bank and what was once the Cinderella Home, which must have provided happy holidays for many children.

Birdwatchers still gather in large numbers at the time of high afternoon tides at the RSPB's Morecambe Bay Reserve, which is reached from a point just over the railway station at Hest Bank. Here, are huge roosts of oyster catcher, dunlin, knot, redshank and shelduck.

Before continuing to describe the changing fortunes of Morecambe as a major seaside resort, it is best to describe how the birds may well provide the salvation of the area. Those in charge of Morecambe until a new vibrant regime took over in the early 1990s, often tried and always failed to copy Blackpool. The latter is too unique, too powerful and too astute to hand over its mantle to anyone else, so why try? Blackpool offers "popular" entertainment morning, noon and night. For almost the whole of its existence Morecambe has been searching for its own identity and has, we believe, now found it. The Lakeland hills overlook the Bay, which is one of Europe's prime natural resources and which has therefore massive appeal. It has a major advantage over its brasher and noisier neighbour in that its wildlife is always more varied and more numerous in winter. Indeed, it is of international importance as a feeding and roosting area.

Bird statues.

The birdwatching is always free and "Tern", which is the title given to the Morecambe Bay Art Project, has recently given nature more than a helping hand. The project is developing into a huge open air sculpture park. At each of the landscaped road roundabouts into the town statues of birds have been set up which lead to the refurbished area on and around the Old Stone Jetty. Many modern towns have made the mistake of commissioning works of modern art which would take a genius to interpret. Morecambe's planners have resisted this, and the exhibits show stunningly accurate interpretations of British seabirds including gannets, guillemots and cormorants.

We once had the pleasure of interviewing the late Eric Morecambe who was always full of fun but he took his birdwatching very seriously. His statue graces Morecambe and it is fitting that his binoculars also should be illustrated. In the field of wildlife Morecambe was also very Wise.

On the Stone Jetty itself are yet more life-like statues, and a number of "pavement games" all with an ornithological theme have been produced. Our last visit was on a glorious autumn morning and as we walked along the Stone Jetty via the Midland Hotel we saw children learning their natural history at the same time as having fun. Beyond the exhibits we watched living cormorants, red breasted mergansers and great crested grebes all catching fish. Local anglers, including some in wheelchairs, were also enjoying good sport and "serious" birdwatchers were all gasping in praise of Morecambe's resurgence. More of this revival later but we must now return to the history of the resort from its zenith to its lowest ebb, and then onward to its next flood tide.

By the 1870s Morecambe was growing fast, but there was still a great reluctance to refer to it by its present name and it was often advertised as the:–

"Gravesend of Lancaster. It is much frequented
by the trippers from the busy towns of Lancashire,
for whose recreation are provided abundant
entertainments of a distinctly popular order."

This "popular and perhaps rather vulgar" image was balanced by an ambitious description given in some guide books which list it as "The English Bay of Naples". We have seen both and, apart from the climate, the backdrop of Morecambe bears favourable comparison. In *"The Topography and Directory of Lancaster and 16 miles round"* published in 1881 the town was prepared to use its new name, although it did not become a fully fledged Borough until 1902. The entry notes: *"Poulton-le-Sands, now better known as Morecambe, is a clean, healthy and popular watering place . . . and now contains several streets and handsome terraces, etc., with numerous well appointed shops, hotels, inns and lodging houses for the reception and accommodation of tourists, for whose use there is a large supply of vehicles and pleasure boats. The crescent opposite the bay is a fine range of buildings and there are four first class hotels, several bazaars and the Morecambe Baths, Palace and Aquarium."*

Morecambe also had its own version of Jeckyll and Hyde in the shape of Thomas Ward's Ship Breaking Yard which was situated right on the sea front. Local workmen must have been grateful to be employed during the hard times of the 1920s and 1930s but those responsible for selling the image of a seaside resort must have been somewhat disheartened. Imagine having the din of hammering, clanking, cutting and beating of metal and the sight of rusty coloured water and industrial debris in the centre of an ambitious seaside resort.

We have a feeling, however, that many visitors spent happy hours around Wards watching the breaking up of famous White Star liners including the *SS Majestic*, the wooden warship *HMS Raleigh* and after the First World War of a number of German U-boats, as well as a number of surface vessels. All these, but especially the latter, must have been something of a tourist attraction. So might the foreign merchant ships which also had their graveyard here and which placed Morecambe on the world maritime map, even if it was for a rather sad reason. Wards were obliged to vacate the old harbour by the Morecambe Town Council in July, 1933. At that time, the latter was carrying out extensive and expensive improvements to the promenade, an essential requirement of any resort. The 1930s was among the most ambitious periods in the town's history, and nothing like it has been attempted since until the present programme was set in motion in 1990, and which is designed to continue into and beyond the next century.

Morecambe's sea defences have always been its prime concern and the incentive to construct a substantial curving promenade may have been given impetus by the fiersome storms of 16th March, 1907, and especially by that of 28th October, 1927. Wards, breaking up yard stood in the way of this progress and it eventually had to go.

Morecambe began its life as a seaside resort rather later than most, but this initially gave it a novelty value, which did not go unnoticed or unenvied by Blackpool which is a mere fifteen miles to the south as the crow flies. Blackpool had its Winter Gardens and Morecambe tried hard to compete with and perhaps surpass it in its elegance. A building was begun in 1876 and was named "The People's Palace", but this soon proved unequal to the demand and in 1896 a new complex was completed which included an aquarium and what was described as Exotic Baths. One of our maiden aunts once referred to these as the "erotic" baths! Nobody got confused with the name Winter Gardens which had a much better ring to it than the Peoples Palace, especially after the events in Russia following the 1917 Revolution.

Morecambe also advertised itself as a spa town providing liberal doses of spring water, but some degree of poetic licence was employed, since the mineral rich liquor was brought in from the limestone knoll at Humphrey Head near Cartmel which had long been famous for its Holy Well. The monks of the nearby priory made good profits from the 'Pilgrims Well' and its properties were renowned at least from the twelfth century onwards. The well is still there and its foul taste is still drank by those who feel that all good medicine must have an unpleasant taste!

Following the turn of the 20th century, there was a severe decline in many seaside resorts and Morecambe's Winter Gardens felt the effects more than most. In 1906 insult was added to injury when the whole complex was purchased by the Broadhead Variety Circuit based, of all places, at Blackpool. The theatre area changed hands in 1933, but continued to thrive and in 1937 the directors were able to buy adjoining land, some of which was sold to Littlewoods and Woolworths who built impressive stores. And then, of course, there was the adjacent money-spinning fairground.

In 1953 Moss Empires Ltd bought control of theatre, ballroom and restaurant plus car park and fairground. The Floral Hall built in 1938 played its part and at one time looked set fair to become a major conference centre.

During the 1970s and 1980s a severe depression set in around most British seaside resorts which had failed to anticipate package holidays to the sun, and had been so short sighted that no repairs were made to existing buildings and no new structures were planned.

Morecambe IIlluminations, 1965.

Morecambe fared worse than the majority of the resorts but the Winter Gardens, according to Jim Trotman the town's Tourism Officer and also to Ken Stancliffe, the owner of the complex, looks set for a major facelift during the late 1990s. The building will now sensibly be known as the Victoria Pavilion. Resorts these days need to plan to entertain visitors for the whole year and this will be reflected in the new development.

As youngsters in the 1940s, Morecambe was near enough to our homes to be within easy reach of a day trip by rail or motor coach. The parks always seemed to be a mass of colour and the resort a hive of activity. For those who stayed late there might be a famous dance band playing on the pier, one of which was led by Mr. Scott who became the husband of Thora Hird. The illuminations, especially around Happy Mount Park, were our equivalent of Disneyland.

Morecambe illuminations, 1969.

Regents Park opened on 17th July, 1926, and is still famous for the excellence of its bowling greens. Until the mid 1890s this site was as near to the "Naughty Nineties" as genteel Morecambe could aspire. Here was the entertainment centre of the new resort and "the summer gardens", as the area was called, even had its own racecourse surrounded by a wide ditch which was used as a skating rink in winter.

We have always felt that we do not make the most of our seaside resorts during winter — many people go abroad in search of a winter wonderland. Morecambe is ideally suited to make use of the backdrop of the Lakeland hills, and the nearby Yorkshire Dales can also be particularly attractive in the winter.

The "summer gardens" had a complex of cafés, a ballroom, a circus, boating pool and an aquarium and may well have been named to compete with the cooler sounding Winter Gardens. It did not succeed, however, and the site crumbled gradually away from the 1890s onwards and this along with Ward's shipyard may have kept discerning tourists away from Morecambe. The site was purchased by the Corporation in the 1920s for £25,000 and converted into a splendid park.

The competition with Blackpool was always intense and in response to the Fylde coasts tower Morecambe attempted to build two, but never aspired to construct more than two piers whereas Blackpool eventually had three! Perhaps there was an intention to build three at Morecambe as the one recently demolished was actually called the Central Pier.

Morecambe's first tower was sited close to the promenade Railway Station, which itself is now being refurbished as a visitors centre and restaurant complex and is at the hub of the recent ambitious rebuilding programme. This first tower was a rather flimsy revolving structure which soon had to be demolished. A much more ambitious but equally unsuccessful effort was built beyond the Central Pier on a site now occupied by Gala Bingo and close to the old village of Poulton-le-Sands.

The Morecambe Tower Company, formed in 1898 with a capital of £70,000 laid out their plans in a lavish prospectus which envisaged:

> *"A tower 232-feet high upon a scale somewhat in excess as regards to attractiveness and different in construction to the towers of Blackpool and Paris. The tower will have a diameter of about 150 feet at the base gradually diminishing to a platform 52 feet in diameter at the summit, upon which will be a large refreshment saloon. A spiral road round the outside will gradually ascend by easy gradients from the ground to the platform, which may also be reached by an electronic tramway or hydraulic lifts. The greater proportion of the first circuit of the spiral roadway will represent an oriental thoroughfare or market place being provided with shops, cafes etc on each side."*

It is a pity that this extravaganza was never completed due to lack of funding, and the final stages of the tower had to be reached by ladders. It was soon struck by lightning and during World War I the upper steelworks were cut up and melted down to produce armaments. The pavilion, originally designed to seat 5,000 people, remained a focal point for visitors in search of "popular entertainment" and was not finally demolished until 1959 when the site was levelled. On it was built a structure now an amusement and bingo hall and of a much more functional but far less appealing shape.

Central Pier, the last of the two to survive, was built in 1869 but destroyed by fire in 1933. The New Central Pier Company rebuilt the structure and incorporated a theatre, dance hall, bars and amusement arcades and for a while it was the most important visitor attraction in the resort. The nearby and so called Super Swimming Stadium was just that and the Midland Hotel, also built at this time, was the height of fashion. On 6th January,

Central Pier in its heyday, the early '70s.

Central Pier after being fire-ravaged on 6th January 1992.

1992, fire again gutted the pier and ambitious but hardly realistic schemes were put forward to rebuild it. The days of pier entertainment are now, however, assigned to history, the modern visitor needs more sophisticated and larger scale entertainment. The late 1970s and early 1980s saw Morecambe at a low ebb and became the butt of comedians "I went to Morecambe last Bank Holiday" quipped one "but it was shut".

This period saw the disappearance of the last of the piers and was indeed the resort's Darkest Hour. Because of pressure from conservationists and also lack of visitors Marineland, was situated near the Old Stone Jetty, which featured dolphin displays also closed down and has now been dismantled. Improving standards, essential these days, meant that the building did not meet the necessary criteria. The pools were too small, conditions in which the stock were kept were falling behind what was required, and the attraction had run its course and was closed. Even the once proud Midland Hotel, used as a film set for many an episode of Agatha Christie's Poirot films, has fallen into decay and apathy and the idea of operating theme weekends never caught on. Its 1930s decor is fading fast.

If we had written this chapter in 1993 it could literally have been subtitled "The Rise and Fall of the Morecambe Empire". The town, however, is now vibrant with hope, and there are many impressive deeds as well as words. The local newspaper is not having to defend Morecambe and the town's Tourism staff are able to silence critics and prepare visitors' brochures which can enthuse not just about the distant past and remote future but boast of the present as well.

We have already mentioned the restoration of Old Stone Jetty and its bird statues as well as the Promenade Station which is now a developing visitors' centre. A new railway station is operating a few hundred yards away close to the recently completed Morrisons Supermarket. Building is going on quickly in this area to produce new amenities, theatres, bars and shopping.

Frontierland Western Theme Park has already spent £4m on redevelopment and in the summer of 1995 they opened the Polo Tower. This is able to carry visitors high up around the outside of a revolving platform. The view from the top reveals Morecambe Bay and the Lakeland mountains at their best. The platform then slowly revolves to reveal the theme park and also the vast building projects which are on going; funded by Central government, local money and with the possiblility of the National Lottery providing additional funds.

The dolphins and their trainer, Peter Williams, at Marineland in 1965.

The Old Floral Hall, so long a popular conference venue, has been given an extensive, expensive and imaginative facelift and now has a wine bar and night club. The Empire Buildings, once doomed to extinction, is now redeveloped as a leisure and shopping complex. In 1995 a new superbowl opened and an impressive yacht club is also in operation

Storms will always buffet the bay and the devastations caused in 1977, 1983 and 1990 will not soon be forgotten. New breakwaters are planned and the section between the Battery and the site of the old West End Pier has already been completed.

In recent years English resorts have reacted to the lack of hot sunshine by providing indoor sun traps, swimming and leisure pools. Morecambe's Dome/Bubbles water complex is one of the best to be found in any resort, and the substantial investment is already proving popular with the sun seekers. 1995 saw the value of investing in outdoor and indoor amenities with bars, cafes, barbecues, tropical indoor pools and an outdoor pool with tiled floors which really do look like sand. Towels and costumes can be hired by those who come on the spur of the moment and the single price of admission allows all the facilities to be enjoyed throughout the day. There are supervised children's activities which means that parents are able to relax.

The Polo Tower.

We have always loved Happy Mount Park and remember the thrill of our own first visit in the 1940s, and later on seeing our son enjoy the Wombles exhibition in the 1960s. The pity is that Mr. Blobby did not survive his period in Morecambe but there is life after Crinkly Bottom; a local businessman Nick Westwell has proved to be a master of illuminations and his recent Emerald Adventure scenes have given back the park's credibility.

Any resort's success depends upon the quality of its beach and pressure has been put on North West Water but who already had on-going plans to produce good-quality bathing water by 1997. All this activity, and the historic city of Lancaster on its doorstep, is bound to attract more visitors to Morecambe and this must therefore provide continued incentives to hotel owners, and other private investors, to view the resort as an opportunity for profit rather than an area of certain disaster.

In the past, Morecambe has always been at pains to provide facilities at least equal to that provided by other resorts. It seldom, however, played its trump card which to be honest has always been its scenic beauty.

Developers during the 1990s have come to realise the value of the tourist potential of the natural world. This is why Morecambe could yet take its place as the North West's most important resort. This time it shows no sign of wasting its unique opportunity.

Morecambe and the rest of the North West seaside resorts are all showing signs of becoming part of Lancashire's developing tourist industry.